man,
master
of his destiny

Cover illustration: a crystal.

ISBN 0-911857-01-X

Published and Distributed by
PROSVETA U.S.A. P.O. Box 49614
Los Angeles, CA 90049-0614

Omraam Mikhaël Aïvanhov

man,
master
of his destiny

Translated from the French

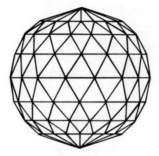

Collection Izvor
No. 202

EDITIONS PROSVETA

CONTENTS

EDITOR'S NOTE

The reader is asked to bear in mind that the Editors have retained the spoken style of the Maître Omraam Mikhaël Aïvanhov in his presentation of the Teaching of the great Universal White Brotherhood, the essence of the Teaching being the spoken Word.

They also wish to clarify the point that the word *white* in Universal White Brotherhood, does not refer to colour or race, but to purity of soul. The Teaching shows how all men without exception (universal), can live a new form of life on earth (brotherhood), in harmony (white), and with respect for each other's race, creed and country... that is, Universal White Brotherhood.

1

THE LAW OF CAUSE AND EFFECT

I

Man cannot perform the slightest act without inevitably triggering certain forces which, just as inevitably, produce certain effects. This notion of the relation of cause to effect was primordial in the original meaning of the word *karma*. It was only later that karma was taken to mean the debt incurred by past misdeeds.

Karma-yoga, one of the many different yogas which exist in India, is nothing more than a discipline which teaches individuals to develop themselves through disinterested activities destined to set them free. It is when man acts with covetousness, cunning and dishonesty that he begins to incur debts and it is then that karma takes on the meaning which is now commonly attributed to it: punishment for faults committed in the past.

In point of fact it would be true to say that karma – in the second sense of the word – becomes operative every time there is action which is not quite perfect, and this means, of course, almost always! But man proceeds by trial and error. He needs to practice before he can do something perfectly and as long as he goes on making mistakes, he has to correct and make up for them and this entails hard work and suffering.

You will perhaps be tempted to conclude that since we inevitably make mistakes in all our actions and that this entails suffering and reparation, it would be far better to do nothing! Not at all. One must act. It is true, of course, that you will suffer, but you will learn, you will evolve, and then one day you will suffer no more. Once you have learned to work correctly there will be no more karma for you. It is a fact that every gesture, every word, triggers certain forces which lead to certain consequences. But if your words and gestures were inspired by lovingkindness, purity and altruism, they would trigger beneficial effects. This is known as *dharma*.

Dharma is the result of well-ordered, harmonious and beneficial actions. Someone who is capable of acting in that way frees himself from the dominion of fate and falls under the law of Providence. It is no good trying to avoid trouble and suffering by avoiding all action; the best way is to be active, dynamic and full of initiative but, instead of acting from egoism and self-interest, to act only from higher motives. This is the only way to avoid disastrous consequences. It is utterly impossible to escape consequences: one way or another there are bound to be causes and consequences whatever you do. The thing to remember is that if you manage to act unselfishly, then the consequences will not be painful but joyful and happy and liberating.

If you choose to do nothing in the hope of being left in peace, you will never develop or learn, you will never earn any rewards; you will make no mistakes, but you will be a stone. Stones never make mistakes! It is far better to make mistakes and even to get a bit dirty, but to learn something. If you have a building full of workmen how can you expect not to find plaster or splashes of paint on the floor? It is asking the impossible. The splashes have to be expected and they don't matter as long as the work gets done and the building goes up. Once the house is finished and all the dirty work done, then you can scrub and polish, and change into your tidy clothes. But at least the job is done.

One day, the Master Peter Deunov said, "I give each one of you a little book on how to learn your alphabet (in Bulgarian we say: *boukvartché*. Perhaps you would say a First Reader). A year later, when I ask you for it, some of you give it back in perfect condition, absolutely clean and new. Having never opened it, they have learned nothing. Others on the contrary, give it back to me stained, marked and dog-eared. They have opened and closed it hundreds of times, they have carried it with them everywhere, they have eaten over its open pages. Yes, but now they can read!" And the Master concluded, "I prefer the second category." I remember I was very young at the time and I shyly asked him which category I was in. "You?" he said, "you're in the second category." I was delighted because I had understood that it was better.

Well, I don't know what condition the *boukvartché* was in when I gave it back to him, but in any event he put me into the category of those who want to get the job done... and he was right. It doesn't matter how many mistakes you make, how many stains you get on your book or how much paint you splash about. It doesn't matter if people criticize you or swear at you, all that is of no importance. What does matter is that you learn to read, to get the job done, to finish building your house. People who are always cautious and afraid to commit themselves never make any progress. Where will all that caution get them?

In the Apocalypse it is written that we must be either hot or cold, not lukewarm, for the Lord "spews out the lukewarm." How is it that some people seem to prefer to be lukewarm? There is no room for such people. You must never be afraid of making mistakes. If you want to learn a foreign language and are so frightened of making a mistake that you never open your mouth, you will never learn! And it is just the same with karma: you must not be paralysed by the fear of making mistakes which you will have to pay for. Gradually, as you practice and learn to act from a divine motive, you will attract not the negative effects of karma, but the positive effects of dharma: an abundance of grace and blessings.

II

No one can evade the law of cause and effect. It is utterly impossible. What is possible, and extremely important, is to know what kind of forces one is unleashing by one's acts. And this is why I say that the most marvellous law given to us by the Cosmic Intelligence, can be found where no one ever thinks of looking for it, where scholars, theologians and philosophers never look anymore: in nature, and in particular in agriculture. Yes, I mean it: agriculture. Every farmer knows that if you plant a fig-tree you will not get grapes from it, that an apple tree will produce apples, not pears. And there you have it, the greatest of all moral laws: "As you sow so shall you reap."

Farmers were the first moral philosophers, it was they who first understood that the intelligence of nature had decreed this stern and immutable law: the law of cause and effect. Later, when they observed the lives of mankind, they found that the same law applied: if you behave with cruelty, selfishness and violence, sooner or later you will be a victim of your own cruelty, selfishness and violence. This law is also known as the law of echo, or the boomerang effect. The ball you hit bounces back and hits you.

"As you sow so shall you reap." If you study this basic law closely you will see how far-reaching it is. It becomes a deeply meaningful system, for all the essential truths can be applied in all areas of life. A detailed understanding of this law can engender a whole philosophy and that is why there are now so many rules and regulations in religion. At the origin of all these rules is one law: you can only reap what you have sown. Other laws equally true have been added to this one, extending and enlarging it into a full-fledged philosophy, and Jesus' words, "Do not unto others what you would not have them do to you," are simply an application of this one law.

Those who try to deny or reject these basic laws become more and more estranged from Truth: their souls are torn by doubt and anxiety, they are forever tossed about on the storms of life. And yet the truth is very simple, it is staring them in the face. Why do modern thinkers refuse to see it and persist in offering their own theories, invented in utter disregard of Cosmic Intelligence? As they no longer believe in a moral law based on the laws of nature, their reasoning is false, the conclusions

they reach are false. Those who read their books
and are gullible enough to accept their teaching,
fall into the same error and end up in a terrible
state of anguish and darkness. So, take care! You
have to learn to reason and make judgments. If you
have no criteria to guide you, you can be led into
error by the first person who comes along. Be on
your guard and don't let yourself be influenced by
clouded human intellects. Follow the guidance of
the Intelligence which has so marvellously ordered
and arranged everything.

Even if you do not believe in God you cannot
fail to recognize that there is an order in nature
and, consequently, that there must be an intelligence which created that order. Reflect for a moment on the fact that each seed reproduces its own
kind. How is it possible not to see that this must be
the work of a higher intelligence? The mere recognition of this law is enough to make us change our
vision of the world. You may not believe in God,
but you cannot deny the fact that every seed produces its own kind exactly, whether it be a plant, a
tree, an insect, an animal or a man. This law is absolute and it should cause you to reflect. You may,
perhaps, allow yourself to be ungrateful, unjust,
cruel or violent, but if you do, you must know that
sooner or later this law will catch up with you and
you will see its application in your own life. If you
have children, for instance, they will resemble you

and through them you will suffer from your own behaviour. Even if God does not exist, you have endless proof of the fact that a Cosmic Intelligence exists.

You go on doing whatever you like, and you believe that you will never have to suffer the consequences: well, believe what you like, nothing will alter the fact that Cosmic Intelligence has already recorded everything you do. You have put a seed, a germ, in every single thought, feeling or act, and the seed grows: if you have been ungrateful, unjust, cruel and violent, one fine day you will come up against the same ingratitude, the same injustice, the same cruelty and the same violence. They will bounce back and strike you, twenty, thirty or forty years later, and when this happens, you will begin to understand that Cosmic Intelligence does, indeed, exist and that everything is recorded. If you want to ignore the Bible and the Gospels, the Prophets, the churches and the temples, you are perfectly free to do so, but you must, at least, give credence to this absolutely irrefutable law: "As you sow so shall you reap." "Sow the wind and reap the whirlwind," said the sages of old who knew how things worked. As for the scholars and thinkers of today who reject this truth, well, they too will find themselves cornered and stricken one day. It is inevitable. They cannot escape the consequences of their acts and, perhaps, when this hap-

pens, they will understand. If they are so intelligent, how is it they cannot see something so simple
and obvious? I will go so far as to say that if you
take this law as your starting point, it is possible to
reconstruct all the sacred books the world has ever
known, just from this one law.

A lot of people say, "It's all very well, the Bible,
the Gospels, say thus and so, but we don't even
know for sure that God exists." I would like to tell
these people that they need not bother their heads
about the existence of God, they do not need to
know if Jesus really lived nor if the Gospels are
authentic, all they need do is recognize this one
law. It is enough to make everything fall into
place: it leads to the Truth. You see, my explanation is very simple. Even if God did not exist, this
law would make it necessary to invent Him! So
why should you be led up the garden path by so-
called fashionable thinkers who undermine everything? Instead of helping human beings to recognize the simple truths which are visible to the
naked eye, they are forever leading them astray
with their "original" ideas. Even if their theories
are utterly in contradiction with the truth that is
written into the whole of nature, that makes no difference: as long as they are new and original everyone is bewitched!

Moral law is a reality, only human beings fail to
see it and continue to argue about God or points of

theology. It is pointless to argue. The only thing that matters is to know that everything is recorded. Absolutely everything. If Nature has so ordained things that a tree records in its seed all its properties, its colour and dimensions and the taste and perfume of its fruit, why should it not be the same for man? Nature has succeeded in recording everything, and the moral law is based on this: nature's memory. You may be astonished, but yes, nature has a memory and nothing can ever efface what it has once recorded. It will be just too bad for the person who decides to discount this memory! Day and night, it records the cacophony, the disorder that reigns within him and one day he will be crushed, struck down, wiped out. No one can escape this law. No one has ever had the power to escape it, be he emperor or dictator... no one! In nature's memory everything is on record. So, be careful. Whatever you do, think or wish, is recorded in the depths of your own cells and one day, sooner or later, you will reap the harvest in your own life. You can create another destiny for yourself only if you take care not to sow the seeds of darkness and destruction through your words, your thoughts and your acts.

You must not believe that those who are kind and generous and full of love, get only knocks in return. People who are in too much of a hurry to draw their conclusions spread this stupid idea that if you are too kind it will only bring you suffering. This is simply not true. Good always produces good and evil always produces evil. If you do good you will receive it in return, whether you want to or not. If you do good and receive evil in return it is because there are still people on this earth who abuse your kindness and try to profit from it; if you are patient and persevere, sooner or later they will be punished, eliminated by someone who is stronger and still more violent, and then they will understand and repent and come to you to atone for all the wrong they did you. And so, good always bears fruit, in fact, it bears fruit twofold, because in cases like this, Heaven counts in your favour all that you suffered in doing what was right, all the undeserved misfortunes that befell you, and your reward will be double.

Today, men stand in dire need of complete, truthful and incontestable knowledge and it is this knowledge that I bring you. Go ahead, try to deny that you reap whatever you have sown! Of course, everyone is convinced for the physical plane, but that is not enough. If they looked a little further and a little higher, they would find the same law at work on all levels. For the world is one, and on every level and at every stage the same phenomena can be found, although always in different, more subtle forms.

Whatever you find in earth can be found also in water. And whatever is in water exists in air, and so on. All four elements obey the same laws, but as their essence and their density are not the same you will find some differences in the way they apply those laws. They react more or less rapidly, more or less violently, but they are governed by identical principles. Man's mind, for instance, is analogous with air: the eddies and currents of the mind are the same as those of the atmosphere, only in the subtler form of ideas and thoughts. The laws governing the psychic plane are identical with those which govern nature.

When a gardener fails to find something in his garden which he did not plant, instead of being furious or revolted, he thinks, "Well, old man, you never had time to sow any carrots, so now you will not have any carrots. Never mind, you will have plenty of lettuce and onions and parsley, because you sowed them." Human beings seem to be very knowledgeable about agriculture, when it comes to fruit or vegetables they know exactly how things work, but as soon as they get into the area of the soul or the mind all their learning vanishes and they think they can reap happiness, joy and peace although they have sown nothing but violence, cruelty and malice. Don't you believe it! All they will reap is the same violence, cruelty and malice

and if they storm and rage, all it proves is that they
are not good farmers!

The very first rule of moral law is never to allow
yourself a thought, a feeling or an action that could
be harmful or dangerous to someone else, because
you will be obliged, one day, to eat their fruit, and
if they were poisonous it is you who will be poi-
soned! The day you begin to take this as an absolute rule you will be on the path to perfection. Of
course, I know that what misleads people is the fact
that these laws take so long to show their effects:
neither reward nor punishment comes at once. One
man may transgress all the laws and yet succeed in
everything he undertakes, whereas another who is
perfectly honest, always doing good, has endless
difficulties: so everyone draws the conclusion that
there is no justice. Human beings do not know why
reward and punishment are so long in coming.
When they think about it, they wonder if it would
not be much better if the effect of the laws made
themselves felt at once, so that they would understand at once.

Let me tell you why the effects of our acts are so
long in coming. As you will see, it is just one more
proof of the lovingkindness and mercy of Cosmic
Intelligence. It is to give men time to learn from experience, to reflect, even to repent and improve,
thereby wiping out past mistakes. If punishment
was meted out at once we would be annihilated and

would never have a chance to improve. Heaven gives us the time we need, sending us a few little problems along the way to encourage us to think, and to give us a chance to make reparation.

Neither are those who do only good rewarded immediately. And it is better so, for if they received their reward at once they might slacken and begin to transgress all the laws. Heaven leaves them time to get stronger and to consolidate their gains, to know themselves better. They are not rewarded at once as a test, to see how long they will continue to persevere in doing good. So, you see, there are good reasons for the delay. But, make no mistake about it, good always produces good fruit, this is an absolute truth. And evil always ends badly, and this is also absolute! The only question is how long it will take for a cause to produce its effects.

It is obvious that one needs great power and strength, willpower, determination, and unshakeable faith to continue to do only good when everything all around one is disintegrating. And it is precisely this that is meritorious. In ideal conditions it is too easy to believe in the power of good and to continue to behave accordingly. Everything is easy, agreeable and beneficial. It is when everything is getting worse and worse that there is great merit in continuing to do good without allowing the conditions to undermine one. A disciple, a Master, endeavours to rely always on the power of his own spirit, even in the midst of the very worst conditions he will always try to summon the forces within him, of righteousness and light. This is the mark of the true spiritualist. If you judge from their words, many people could pass for spiritualists, but the least little inconvenience bowls them over completely. Where is their power of spirit?

Everybody would like others to be thoughtful, friendly, patient and indulgent with them. That is normal, but how do you go about obtaining it? By being thoughtful, friendly, patient and indulgent oneself! If you want people to behave well towards you, you have to behave well towards them first. You will surely say, "Oh, we know all that." Yes, you know all that, but only in theory. There are still millions of people in the world who are rude, hard and cruel, and who are surprised and hurt when others behave in the same way to them, they are convinced that it is the others who should submit and comply with their wishes. Just look at the way they behave: they expect to get satisfaction by means which are the exact opposite of what they are looking for and, at the same time, they simply do not believe that if they sowed gentleness, love and kindness around them, they would be treated with gentleness, love and kindness. Yet I assure you, even if someone is disagreeable and unkind to you, if you continue to send him only good things, after a while he will give in.

If you want to receive affection and trust, you have to call for them. I can hear you say, "I keep calling for them and they don't come!" No, when I say call for them, I mean you have to summon them from within yourself. You have to produce them. When you produce good things in yourself you can be one hundred percent sure you will find them in others too. It is when you produce them in yourself that you attract them to you. That is the magic of it. Why not give it a try? If you want to receive something you are very fond of, try first of all to give it to others. You cannot receive what you have not given. You may say, "That's not true. Look at all the bigwigs who are rich and important and who give nothing, they're cold and contemptuous and yet they receive respect and esteem and honours from all sides." That is simply because they have honoured others in a previous incarnation, so now it is their turn to receive honours. But if they continue to be haughty and unloving, they will end by receiving the same treatment from others later on.

The secret of success, the secret of true happiness, is to show in your own behaviour what you want to receive from others. To smile and receive a smile in return is such a little thing: you gave a smile and it was returned! You have been kind and friendly to someone and he has been kind and friendly to you. Good! You have exchanged civilities and that is excellent, it is necessary, and it makes you feel good! But you must apply the same law in other areas to trigger results far more important than a smile, a handshake, a friendly glance, or some kind words in passing. You can shake the whole universe with this law, and this is where it becomes really interesting: to be able to go far, far away and influence great areas in space....

You can only reap fruits which correspond to the seeds you have sown. Now, of course, there may be all kinds of bad weather: the sun may have been too hot and may have burnt all the crops, maybe there was a drought or birds and moles have eaten all your seeds. That is another question. Those are simply accidents which change nothing of the reality of the law. The innate properties of the seed cannot be taken away. It can be prevented from bringing forth fruit, but nothing can alter its nature. And that is what I am talking about: the nature of the seed.

So, if you are always very friendly and polite and all you get in return is four-letter words, no matter! That is a detail! Besides, you have to see who treats you like that and when and in what circumstances. Perhaps you have been too kind, too charitable and generous and too trusting and you have probably been pigeonholed as an imbecile and you will just have to put up with the transitory conventions of humanity. But this does not mean a thing, it will not last. People and circumstances are always changing but the law does not change. When true values are restored, everything will fall into place once again and you will receive the good that you have sown.

In the world as it is today, you have to be tough to be appreciated. You have to ride rough-shod over others and be aggressive and thoroughly unpleasant. If you do this people think you are somebody worthwhile! But this will not last forever. Sooner or later another tough character will come along and it will be your turn to take a thrashing. You must not let yourselves be impressed by a situation which is only temporary: if you notice, you will see that people who are violent always end by being ill-treated by others more violent than they.

So, do not be in too much of a hurry to find all kinds of objections. I know all the possible objections you can make far better than you do. I never wait for other people to object, "Yes, but why this and why that?" I seize my own arguments by the throat and shake them and if they stand up to my attacks, then I know that they are gold, pure gold! And if they are gold, then they are the truth. What about arguments which cannot stand up to such rough treatment? It only remains to bury them deep and dark. R.I.P. Problem solved!

Now, let me paint a picture for you: imagine a vast and magnificent forest full of birds and ani-

mals and trees loaded with all kinds of fruit and
flowers, a forest bursting with good things! But
there is just one snag: it is surrounded by a very
high, very thick wall, which means no one can get
in. There is even broken glass and barbed wire on
the wall and as if that were not enough, the forest is
full of dangerous animals: bears, lions and tigers
who ask nothing better than to dine off the impru-
dent intruder. The problem is that you need some
of that lovely fruit. How can you get at it? All of a
sudden you notice some monkeys in the trees and
you know you are saved. You take a bag of oranges
and you go close to the wall and start pelting the
monkeys with your oranges. In no time at all, as
monkeys are very good mimics, they start picking
fruit from the trees to throw back at you and before
long you have all the fruit you need, you can fill
your basket and go home! The secret is to throw
oranges at the monkeys!

You will say, "What on earth is all that about?
As though we could go to a forest and throw
oranges over the wall at the monkeys!" But it is an
image. Have you never seen a sower in a field? He
is throwing oranges at the monkeys, only, in this
case, the oranges are minute and the monkeys are
hidden under the surface of the soil. When the
sower has finished he can go away in peace of
mind, and when he comes back a few months later,
he only has to reap the harvest and fill his granary.

"Oh, all right," you may say, "if that's all it is, we have understood." I doubt it. You still have not interpreted it correctly. The monkeys are the forces of nature, whether under the soil or in the trees makes no difference. It is a symbol. And now, for the explanation: the universe created by God is an immense forest bursting with treasures. The walls are all the obstacles which prevent men from reaching those treasures. The monkeys are the entities of the hidden world and the oranges are the light and love that you decide to spread round by your thoughts and feelings. And then what happens? Well, once you start throwing your oranges, the entities of the hidden world do the same, they send you the fruit from the forest trees, that is to say, blessings of all kinds, and they send you a hundredfold what you send others. But if you send them hatred, bitterness and anger, then, one day, that is what will be thrown back at you.

"As you sow so shall you reap," and this also means that your present behaviour directly prepares your future. Every instant, by the inner work you do, you can give direction to your future; every decision you make for good or ill, orients your future for good or ill.

Just suppose that today you decide to serve God, to help your fellow men, to overcome the bad influence of your lower self: at once, your future becomes beautiful, full of light and power. All the marvels of creation are in store for you. Why are you unable to experience them at once? Because the past still has a hold on you. But if you work faithfully, always maintaining the same decision, always heading in the same direction, little by little the past will be paid off and one day you will come into your divine inheritance. If you decide to live a selfish life again, everything will be changed again and you will begin to store up for yourself another future, full of suffering and disillusion, even though in the present you will go on having fun and putting through your business deals. Your present will be the same because you still have some reserves and you cannot see the dark future awaiting you. But once your reserves run out, that horrible future will be on you all at once. It is easy to create the future but it is very difficult to erase the past.

Let me give you another image: you want to take a trip and you are trying to decide where to go: Nice or Moscow. Let's say you decide to go to Nice. From then on, the way you will go is predetermined, the countryside you see on your way, your fellow-passengers, the stations your train goes through. Once you decide to go in a given direction, everything has been planned in advance and you have to follow a given route. It is not you who create the countryside you travel through. Its existence does not depend on you, but what does depend on you is the initial choice of direction.

In reality we do not actually create our future. To say that man creates his own future is a manner of speaking, it would be more exact to say that he chooses the direction he wants to go in. You say, "I'll go that way." All right. But it is not up to you to create the regions your route takes you through nor their inhabitants. They have long since been created by God. We do not create our evil fate, but we steer ourselves towards its treacherous quick- sands, and swamps and forests full of danger. We decide only what direction we will go in, that is all. And for a wondrous future the same applies: we decide to go a certain way, but the future is already there, waiting for us. There are thousands of differ- ent regions and spheres in space peopled with an infinite variety of creatures and, depending on what destination we pick, to visit them, we either rise or sink.

Misfortune and happiness already exist, other people have experienced them before us, they were created long ago. It is up to us to choose which way we want to go. And that is why, now, at this min- ute, you must decide to change direction and steer towards the regions of Paradise prepared for you by God, for all eternity.

2

YOU WILL SEPARATE
THE SUBTLE FROM THE GROSS

From childhood, most human beings know that when they want to eat something, fruit, fish, oysters or snails, they have to start by separating the edible parts from the skin and bones, or from the core, pips or shell. When they eat cheese, they automatically leave the crust; they are conscious of the need to eliminate harmful or indigestible elements from their food. In fact they have even invented all kinds of methods designed to do just that: refining, sterilization, pasteurization, etc.

This custom of peeling, separating and rejecting from their food anything dirty or not fit for consumption, is a tremendous step in the evolution which raises man above the animals. The only trouble is that men still have not understood that there are other areas where they should also clean, wash and eliminate, sort out and separate what is valuable from what is worthless, the pure from the impure. On the level of feelings and thoughts, for instance, they are constantly absorbing and digesting a different kind of food... but here, they are still like cats: they swallow the whole mouse including the skin and the guts! In other words, they absorb everything, even what is dirty and harmful. They have some progress to make in learning to sort out the good from the bad in their psychic food, as they have learned to do for their physical food.

It is written in the Emerald Tablet of Hermes Trismegistus, "You will separate the subtle from the gross," which means that you must separate the pure from the impure. Of course, Hermes Trismegistus was not talking about food, even spiritual food, he was talking about the philosopher's stone. But still, the same principle applies. What is pure must be separated from what is impure, just as gold and precious stones have to be separated from their matrix. In fact, the whole of life, all industries and trades are based on the principle of separating or sorting things. Wherever you go, in shops and super-markets, in the diamond and gem trades... things are always being sorted. Exams and competitions are ways of sorting too, whether it be a question of choosing a Commander-in-Chief or this year's Miss World, there is always some sorting and eliminating to be done! But no one seems to realize that in the spiritual life too one has to sort and separate, choose and eliminate. If you ask people, even very well-educated people, which are the harmful thoughts and feelings which cause disease and disintegration in man, they simply do not know. To them, all thoughts and feelings seem to be about the same. They never imagine that here, too, there are distinctions to be made, just as with foods or fuels which are classed according to their quality.

In the past, people used to light and heat their homes with very poor quality fuels which smoked and made one's eyes smart, and smelt so awful one almost suffocated! Nowadays, we use electricity which leaves no waste and produces no smoke. For coal, we now know that there are different qualities, ranging from the kind that gives very little heat and leaves a lot of slag to that which gives a great deal of heat and leaves very little waste. No matter what kind of fuel you use: coal, wood, oil, petrol or straw, it always contains a certain amount of non-combustible material, but in different proportions, and it is this proportion that is interesting. Every material can be classed according to its quality, as better or inferior, and that is why we always have to choose and discriminate. And the same applies to our feelings.

Feelings can be compared to fuels, and as they are not all top quality, they do not all provide the best source of light or heat or motive power. Just as for food, some feelings are "edible" while others must be rejected because they contain some slag or dirt which the astral "stomach" would be unable to

digest. Let's suppose that you are in a rage, a prey
to feelings of jealousy, hatred and revenge. What
happens? Well, there will certainly be a lot of heat,
but there will also be a lot of smoke and a lot of
waste which will poison you. You should know
this! Of course, there is no branch of approved
science which studies humans' feelings with a view
to classing them. Any old feeling is good enough.
Down it goes like a dainty morsel and no one
bothers to wonder what effect it will have on them.
And it is exactly the same with our thoughts: no
one discriminates between what is beneficial and
what is harmful; there is no scale of values by
which to judge them.

All those who believe they should allow even
the most licentious passions or desires to express
themselves without inhibition are in reality ignora-
muses who have never studied human beings and
who do not have the first idea about how they were
created to start with. All they know is that they
have stomachs and sexual organs which, obviously,
have to be catered to! I agree. They must be catered to, but should we not be a little more discrim-
inating all the same? Of course, young people will
say, "No, no. No discrimination," but since they
accept that they have to discriminate in what they
eat, why should they not accept that if they swallow any and every feeling or pleasure without discrimination they will make themselves ill?

Men eat bread, fruit, vegetables, fish, meat, etc., and in the area of feelings, there is as much variety and as many rich foods as in the physical sphere. Some feelings are like pork-butcher's meat: blood-pudding and smoked ham, whereas others are wine or fruit or vegetables. But as human beings know nothing about the world of feelings, they eat whatever takes their fancy and then they fall ill. They must learn not to eat food which poisons them: anger, spite and jealousy and, above all, sensuous love, for that kind of love contains a lot of toxic elements.

Wherever you go you will find that men have countless wants and desires in their hearts. That is one commodity that is never in short supply in the world. But what is in short supply – in fact it is so rare as to be almost non-existent – is the wisdom that would enable men to choose amongst all their desires and to satisfy only those which would not hinder their true development. Although this wisdom is the most precious thing anyone could ever possess, no one wants it. No one seeks it. Why? Because their reasoning is faulty. They think that being wise means giving up certain joys and pleasures, and they have no wish to deprive themselves. This thinking is equivalent to admitting that they are both ignorant and stupid, because in reality, they would be far happier if they had enough wisdom to discern the true nature of their feelings and to sort out the good from the bad. How can they be happy if they are blind? When you cannot see, you cannot take precautions to protect yourself and you are at the mercy of whatever you bump into. Don't imagine that blindness will bring you happiness! It is as though someone handed you a closed bag, full of all kinds of things, saying, "Go ahead, reach in and take whatever you like." Without looking to see what is there you put in your hand and get bitten to death by a snake! Believe me, if you are blind, there will always be a snake that will bite you.

Over and above the physical body, man has other more subtle bodies: etheric, astral, mental, causal, buddhic and atmic. When he gives free rein to his passions he stirs up currents on the astral plane, thereby releasing the monstrous entities which dwell there and, without realizing it, attracts them to come and invade humanity. Man is totally ignorant of his own structure and composition, and of the constant interaction that goes on between human beings and the invisible beings in the other regions of the universe. It is this ignorance which is the cause of his great misfortunes. Whereas the disciple who knows how he has been put together in the Lord's workshops and how he is in constant relationship with the inhabitants of other planes of the universe, becomes aware of the need to pick and choose: he eliminates certain elements, closing his doors to hostile forces and opening them to forces which are beneficial, harmonious and constructive.

My dear brothers and sisters, you must realize that your bodies are composed of the ingredients you absorb and, therefore, if these are impure, you will be impure, if they are harmful, you will fall ill. This is an absolute law, not only on the physical plane but also on the psychic or spiritual plane. Just as you have to be careful to eat food that has been properly cleaned and washed, in the same way, on the level of your thoughts and feelings, you have to be on guard night and day against intruders.

Every country puts customs officers at its ports of entry to check on who goes in and out. If you have no customs officers to stop the dangerous, ill-intentioned visitors from entering your territory, you will be invaded by entities from every region and you will be contaminated. Put customs men at your ports of entry and each time a thought turns up and wants to come in, say, "Wait a minute: where are you from? Show me your colours. What will you bring in with you if I let you in?" In this way you would foresee the catastrophic results of admitting certain thoughts and send them packing.

There is a science to sorting the good from the bad. Thoughts and feelings are not all made of the same materials, there are degrees of purity, and the higher you go to find your materials, the purer they will be. In fact, you can see this, too, on the physical plane: pure materials are lighter and have a tendency to rise, whereas all that is impure is heavy and settles like dregs and mud on the bottom. Also, the purer your materials, the better will they resist wear and tear. This is why you must build your body of the purest materials so as to be able to resist suffering and even death, for if the materials you use are of the very highest quality, suffering and death have no power over them. Disease and death have power only if they can get a hold on something. Even the Devil has no power over you unless he can find weaknesses or vices to hold on to, in other words, unless he finds impure materials in you. If man is afflicted with so many unpleasant circumstances in his life, it is because he allows the forces of evil to get a hold on him and penetrate inside.

I have told you that I do not like to read too many books because the greatest truths in life are not to be found in books written by men, but in the great book of Nature. Everything has been written in that book, and what I am telling you now is drawn from the lessons I have learned from insects: roaches, ants, fleas, etc. When a house is very clean insects are no problem, but as soon as you leave a little dirt about or some remnants of food which begin to rot, then the insects arrive.

How do they know there is something for them to eat, and why are some people bitten by fleas and lice and not others? Because their blood contains impurities which provide excellent food for these little beasties. They only like what is impure, purity has no attraction for them!

If you have no desire to be invaded by roaches or ants, keep your house clean, if you have no desire to be bitten by fleas, purify your bloodstream, and if you do not want to be invaded by harmful spirits, be sure not to prepare food for them. The Gospels recount some instances of creatures possessed by devils. Why had the devils entered those people? Because they found in them the kind of impure nourishment they thrive on. And this is why Jesus, when he chased the devils out, said to the person he had just saved, "Go and sin no more." In other words, "Don't let any impurities into you again."

It is important for man's health and beauty and even for his intelligence that he choose his physical food well, and it is equally important that he choose his spiritual food wisely. His whole future depends on it. It is the quality of what he absorbs that will make him either a superior being or a brute and a criminal.

3

EVOLUTION AND CREATION

From the very first stages of his evolution, man has manifested the urge to create, as we can see from archeological discoveries dating back to the most primitive civilisations. In the same way, from a very early age, children always have the urge to build, draw, paint pictures, etc. One could say that this need to be a creator and, in this way resemble our Heavenly Father, is one of man's most constant and strongest instincts.

Art in all its forms is proof that this urge to create which is common to all human beings, is not restricted to the creation of children, to biological reproduction with a view to ensuring the preservation of the species. The existence of art demonstrates man's need to go beyond himself, to reach forward towards something more beautiful, subtler and more perfect. Man's creative faculties lie on a higher plane than his ordinary level of consciousness. They dwell in a region of his soul which manifests itself as a capacity to explore and contemplate and, finally, to capture the elements of a reality which far surpasses him. To create is to surpass and outstrip one's own limitations.

The reason why certain inventors, for instance, have been able to make such revolutionary discoveries, is that they were able to rise to the realm of imagination and higher still, to that of intuition, and tune in to ideas and images which they then retranscribed and materialized. Modern science has not yet explored the possibilities open to intuition which, like radar or some kind of cosmic radiolocator, can foresee, predict and tune in to the future. From time to time, when a thinker who is half-way between orthodox science and esoteric science, launches new ideas, no one takes him seriously. He is criticized or ridiculed and it is only later on that it becomes evident that he was one of humanity's pioneers.

Man's imaginative power is a truly creative faculty and if he learns to purify it and to cultivate it in perfect clarity and lucidity, it is capable of opening his eyes to realities which he has never dreamt of. All inventors spend long hours plunged in research and meditation and it is undeniable that their intuition is a really authentic faculty. Here in this Initiatic School, we are doing exactly what they do, but consciously, in full awareness of what we are doing. The difference is that our imagination is not aimed at physical, chemical or technical discoveries, but at inner, spiritual discoveries. And we too can discover wonderful things, whose existence many people never even suspect.

As I have already explained, imagination is like the spouse of the inner man, who gives birth to his children. Some of his offspring are a great success and some are a disaster, according to the quality of the seed he supplied. And if his children make mischief and cause damage to property it is the father who is held responsible, it is he who will have to pay a fine, who is liable to be tried and condemned to pay damages in their place. On the other hand, when they win prizes or competitions, it is their father who receives the credit! You will probably say, "But what children are you talking about?" I am talking about our thoughts and feelings. They are our children, each one of us has fathered them. This is a very vast field for study and analysis, but I must not digress, let us get back to the heart of the subject.

This creative instinct, therefore, which we all have, incites us to outstrip our ordinary capacities and puts us in touch with other regions, other worlds filled with subtle and luminous, etheric beings. And it is thanks to that part of ourselves which has gone out from us and reached higher planes where it tunes in to entirely new elements, that we are able to create children who are superior to us, or works of art which surpass our limits.

Very often, a creation is far more beautiful than its creator. Sometimes one sees a funny little man who looks like nothing on earth and one is utterly astonished to discover that he has created some tremendous work of art, worthy of a giant! That subtle part of himself which is capable of travelling very far and very high, has gone out from him and gathered a rich harvest of new elements and when later, he sets to work, he produces something prodigious, something entirely original which fills the whole world with admiration.

Although all men have the creative urge, unfortunately very few are capable of becoming true creators on a spiritual plane, very few rise to this level and realize that, in order to produce sublime works of art, they must know certain laws and apply certain methods. What these methods are you will soon understand.

How is it that the earth which is so dingy, bare and sterile in Winter, is clothed in the Spring with lovely, colourful vegetation: grasses and flowers, trees and fruit? The reason is that, in the Spring the earth is more exposed to the sun and begins to receive certain elements from him. So she sets to work and surpasses herself, producing extraordinary, brightly-coloured works of art and regaling us with the nectars and perfumes she offers to all creatures. Therefore, if man wants to create and produce anything noteworthy he must take a leaf out of nature's book and find a sun, a being more powerful and more intelligent than himself with whom he can unite and interrelate.

Now do you see why we go to see the sunrise in the morning? It is in order to create works which resemble him, works which will be new, transparent, full of light, warmth and life. But, in fact, the sun, in this context, is a symbol: a symbol of God Himself to Whom we turn in order to unite ourselves with Him, for it is thanks to our interrelation with the Lord that we shall ever become creators like Him. Here you have the raison d'être, the true motive of prayer, meditation and contemplation and of all the spiritual exercises. But I am not sure that all this is very clear in your minds, so I shall try to explain it more fully.

For a very long time now I have had a burning desire to go to war against today's materialistic philosophy and eliminate it. You will say, "What ambition! What pride! No one has succeeded so far." No, I know. But I have a few very simple arguments up my sleeve and I am sure that thanks to them, I shall succeed where others have failed! First I take two glasses into which I pour two different perfumes. The glasses remain separate, they are two quite distinct objects. From a materialistic point of view there is no communication between them, and this is perfectly true on the material level. Seen as exterior forms, as containers and noth-

ing more, the two glasses are quite separate. But
this is no longer true if you consider their contents,
for each perfume gives off some subtle particles
which rise and spread into the air and intermingle.
Any science which concerns itself exclusively with
tangible, visible and measurable phenomena
knows nothing of what goes on on the much more
subtle level of invisible emanations and quintes-
sences, and so, on this level, it ceases to be true and
reliable. Half the truth escapes it.

Now, let's consider the sun : he is very far away,
millions of miles away from us and yet we can feel
his presence here on earth. He touches us, he
warms and heals us. How can he be so close in
spite of the distance that lies between him and the
earth? It is because something comes out from
him, a quintessence which is part of him : his rays.
And by means of his rays he establishes the contact. When he embraces us, caresses us and pen-
etrates us we become one with him. And since the
light and warmth of the sun are none other than
the sun himself, we can say that the sun and the
earth touch, that the planets touch each other.
Take our planet : there is the earth, the soil, and
over the earth there is water. Over the water is the
air, and above the air is the ether. It is on that level
that one can say that the planets touch each other.
They are not in contact on the physical, solid level,
but on the subtler level of the soul. And this is why

astrologers have always believed in the influence of the planets and constellations on men's lives.

Now, let us look at those miniature planets and constellations: men and women. What happens between them? Here is a boy and there is a girl: they look at each other and smile. From a purely materialistic point of view, we have here two distinct and separate physical entities and there is no contact between them and therefore no communication. But if you look at the scene from the point of view of a spiritualist, it is quite obvious to you that that is nonsense: the souls of these two young people are in communication with each other. They are really and truly fused into one, by means of their subtle fluids and emanations, in exactly the same way as the rays of two suns in space blend and fuse together.

Perhaps these few words will help you to understand how, by means of his subtle bodies, man has the possibility of reaching out to the Universal Soul and blending into it. This is the reason for prayer. Prayer is nothing more nor less than an interaction with our Creator, an act by which we rise above ourselves in the endeavour to find elements that will help us to create perfect works, divine works. And here again we have an essential element of the cosmic moral law: if an artist wishes to create an unforgettable masterpiece which will last forever, he must take care not to restrict himself to the level of his five senses, as so many contemporary artists do. Nowadays it has become the fashion in the art world to portray the most prosaic and commonplace subjects. Most artists no longer know how to rise above themselves in order to contemplate sublime beauty. They offer their public monstrosities, gargoyles! They have lost the secret of true creativity.

If you aspire to becoming an authentic creator, you must link with the Godhead in order to receive some divine particles which you can then communicate to your creation and, in this way, your child or your work of art will surpass you in beauty and intelligence. So, there you are, dear brothers and sisters, new horizons are being opened up to you: how to establish a link and an interaction between yourself and all those beings who surpass you; how to use prayer, meditation and contemplation as means of creation. There is such a wealth of possibilities in this area that a whole existence would not be enough to explore them all.

Nothing is more important for man than to restore the bond with his Creator. Have you not noticed that the conception of a child is based on the same law: the mother has to be united with the father, become one with him? All creation requires that there be union between a father and a mother. But if the subtler factor, the soul or the imagination, takes no part in the conception, then the higher elements cannot be captured and utilized and the act of creation will fail or if it does not actually fail, it will not produce anything that will be better than the parents. Creation is not something stagnant, simply a reproduction or a copy of something that already exists. It is a step forward, an evolutionary step. This is how each individual advances. In fact, this is how the whole cosmos advances and evolves : thanks to this creative instinct. And with the exception of God Himself, everything must evolve.

4

TWO JUSTICES:
HUMAN AND DIVINE

I

For centuries men have understood that life in society is based on the law of exchange. Experience has taught them that life could be maintained only on condition that each individual takes and gives, gives and takes, and that this applies on all levels of life : physical, psychological and spiritual. This law of exchange is called justice : you take something for yourself and you give its equivalent in exchange. If you can maintain a right balance between what you take and what you give, then you are just.

But people do not bother their heads too much about giving or paying exactly what they owe : they take a lot and they give very little. What they do not realize is that their debts accumulate and are recorded on that tiny tape we all have within us and which records everything we do. One day they will have to pay and this will mean suffering for them. They have eaten and drunk, stolen and abused the love of beings they have seduced or betrayed, and then, because they have managed to get away without paying the bill, they imagine they will never be caught. And this is where they are making a big mistake. It makes no difference if they change their name and address and even their nationality, the Lords of the Karma who dwell on high, have their prints and can trace them. In fact, very often in the same incarnation, they find the person, present the bill and demand payment. Much of the suffering endured by men is simply payment for injustices they have committed.

Justice should be understood as liberation, for only when you have given back or paid for what you have taken are you free. And this is why, at this point, I want to help you to understand the justice which must exist in our relations with our family, with society, with nature, and even with the whole cosmos.

Man receives a great deal from his parents: his body and life itself (let's say, for the sake of argument, that he receives life from them, although in fact, they have not created him but simply transmitted life to him). He receives clothes, food, a home, an education. This means that a considerable debt has accumulated and must be paid. Many children refuse to acknowledge this, they criticize their parents and are always against them. Some even detest them. This is unjust. Their parents have loved them and suffered for them, they have fed, clothed and protected them, nursed them through illnesses and given them an education. So, before anything else, man has a debt towards his parents.

But then man also has a debt towards the society or nation he belongs to, for it has given him a rich heritage of culture and civilisation, with schools, museums, libraries, laboratories, theatres, etc. And society puts all kinds of things at his disposal: trains, ships, airplanes, doctors to take care of him, teachers and professors to instruct him, an army and even a police force to protect him! Then he also owes something to his race, for it has given him not only the colour of his skin but a whole physical and psychological structure – a mentality. But this is not all: he also has a debt to the earth which gave him birth and nourished him with her fruits, to our solar system (because it is thanks to the sun and the planets that we are continually sustained and vivified), to the whole universe, and, finally, to God.

How many people realize that they have never done anything but take, take, take and that now they have a huge debt to pay? Ah, according to them, they owe nothing to anybody. In fact, not only do they think they owe nothing, but they also think they have the right to criticize and demolish anything and everything. What a sorry mentality!

What they do not know is that if they go on like that, they will be wiped off the face of the earth, for Nature cannot tolerate creatures who do not respect her laws: they are a threat to the whole and she eliminates them in one way or another.

A disciple who understands the importance of the law of justice loves first and foremost his parents, and tries to do them only good so as to repay what he owes them. He also gives something back to society, to his country, to mankind, to the solar system, to the whole universe and, finally, to God. What can he give? His work, his thoughts and feelings, his gratitude. Through his activity he is continually sending something good out into the universe. This is how he pays his debts, and nature then recognizes him for an intelligent being. What about all those who do not do this? In nature's eyes they are thieves: dishonest, unjust beings who need to be taught a lesson... which she is well able to do!

To be just therefore, is first and foremost to understand that there are certain laws and that when we take anything from nature: food, air, water, warmth, the sun's rays, we incur a debt. And as we cannot pay this debt with money, we must pay with love, gratitude and respect and with a will to learn what is written in her book. We pay her, too, when we do something good for another creature, when we communicate a little light and warmth to others. Suppose you have a Master who has given you untold treasures: what exactly do you owe him? You cannot pay him in kind, with advice, instruction or consolation. He does not need that from you. It is not he who must be the beneficiary of your good deeds, but others. If you transmit the treasures your Master gives you to other human beings he will be delighted and will consider that he has been paid in full.

We are not obliged to give back the air we breathe or the water we drink in the form of air and water. How would we go about manufacturing air or water, or the warmth and light of the sun's rays? We have received our bodies from the earth and one day it is true, we are going to have to give them back. There is no other way. But in the meantime, as long as we are still living, we keep and use them. No one asks us to give them back. What we can give is light, for man has been constructed in such a way that he is capable of radiating, shining and sending out rays to the whole universe. He has received a quintessence of light which he can continually amplify, vivify and send out into space. But he can do so only on condition that he really works at it and practices, otherwise all that comes out of him is darkness. This is new for you, but remember this: although we are severely limited on the physical plane, on the spiritual plane our possibilities are infinite and we can give what we receive a hundredfold.

You may say that no one has ever explained justice to you in this way before. I know. Human justice is limited to the cases of murder, theft or divorce that come up before the courts. But divine justice is quite another matter and it is this, the only true justice, that you must understand. When, for example, you see that someone detests you, there must be a reason. Try and find out what it is. Perhaps you owe him a debt. Why not try to pay off your debt by doing something for him, either on the physical or on the spiritual plane? If you want to free yourself more rapidly you will have to choose the way of divine justice: kindness, generosity, love and self-sacrifice. In this way, long-standing debts that would take years or even centuries to pay off in other ways, can be paid in full very quickly and, sometimes, immediately.

This is why there are people who accepted to suffer persecution, martyrdom and death: in order to free themselves by paying off the debts accumulated from other incarnations. Those who are truly enlightened choose the quickest route. They are in a hurry and have no desire to stay behind in the lower regions, miserable captives, for longer than necessary. They want to be free and so they accept to suffer.

Of course there are not a great many like this. The majority prefer to get out of paying their debts, still thinking they can avoid them altogether if they are sly enough. Only, there you are, karmic law always catches up with them in the end and obliges them to pay. I know that many of you, listening to me today, will stop up their ears. But the day will come when they will be submerged under the weight of their debts and then they will acknowledge the truth of what I am saying and make up their minds to tot up their own bill, how much they owe and to whom, and to pay it in one form or another. If it is too late to repay their father, for instance, then they can pay their own son or their wife.

Well, there you have the disciple's task: to pay all his debts from now on, and even to pay more than he owes in order to free himself more rapidly. And so, this is what you can work at for the next few days: review your whole life and try to remember how you have behaved, what you have taken without giving in exchange, and from whom. Then, go and find those people, apologize to them and pay them what you owe them or do something for them, saying, "I didn't realize. I was blind. Please forgive me if I made mistakes and accept this or that so that we can be at peace with each other."

And what if you cannot find the people you owe something to because they are no longer on earth? Then you can turn directly to God, saying, "Lord, I understand now for the first time, how un-

just I've been with others. I've cheated them and
imposed upon them. Now it's too late. I can't make
up to them for the wrong I did them, but I do want
to advance. So, please, Lord, here is my life. Take
it. From now on it will be consecrated to your service. It's the most precious thing I possess and I
want you to dispose of it to pay all my debts. You
know far better than I who my creditors are and
how much I owe them. I'm at your service for all
eternity." This is the best possible way to put
everything right. When the Lord sees that you have
reached such a high level of consciousness as to
want to consecrate your life to Him for all Eternity
(and be sure to make it quite clear that it is for
Eternity and not just for this incarnation), He will
be astounded at all the light that flows from you,
He knows very well that if you can feel and say
such a thing it means that you are full of light...
and He is dazzled! And of course, as He does not
want to be outdone by you, He shows Himself to be
even more generous and wipes out many of your
debts, "There, it's finished. Paid in full. We won't
talk about it anymore. Now go and work hard."

For years, when I was young, I implored the
powers above to come to my help, "What can I do?
I'm weak, stupid, ordinary, worthless... do you
really want me to stay that way? I can't be of any
use to you like this. I warn you, you'll have cause
to regret it if you don't help me, so hurry up and

take everything I have. Take my life, if you want, and come and live in me. I can't go on like this. Send me angels. Send me quantities of noble and intelligent beings, full of light and purity. It will be to your advantage. Otherwise I'll only make mistakes and it will be all your fault, because you didn't come and help me when I asked you to." You see? I threatened them! And upstairs, they scratched their heads and said, "Well, of all things! He's really got us in a tight spot." So they discussed it and decided that if they left me as I was, it was quite true, I would only cause a lot of trouble and do a lot of damage, and they decided to give me what I asked for. And now it seems that from time to time, I manage to do something which is not entirely reprehensible!

And now, what about you? Why not make the same request? What are you waiting for? Go ahead and ask. Ah, yes, I know. You are afraid to consecrate your life to God: you want to keep it for yourself. How often have I heard people say, "I'm going to live my own life." That is all well and good, but what kind of life are you going to live, stupid or divine? Everyone wants to "live his own life," and it usually means a life without rhyme or reason.

From now on you should aim at something better. Say, "Lord, I'm beginning to realize that without You, without Your light and intelligence, I'm

worthless: I'm ashamed, disgusted and sick of myself and I'm ready to serve you and to do something
for Your children and for the whole world." Repeat
this day and night. Even if the Lord stops up His
ears because He is tired of listening to you, never
stop! The twenty-four Lords of the Karma will
hold a meeting (I know these meetings and I know
the Chairman too, He is an extraordinary, sublime
being). So, they will hold their meeting and, as you
are continually pestering them with your plea, they
will publish a decree to be proclaimed throughout
all the regions of space, declaring that from such
and such a date, at such and such a time, a change
will take place in your life. The angels and all the
faithful servants of God will set to work to apply
this decree at once and, sure enough, you will see
that something really does change in your destiny.

II

Most people have not yet attained mastery over their own impulses. If they have been disappointed by someone, they do all they can to destroy his reputation and make life unbearable for him. If he falls ill or even attempts suicide, they never stop to wonder if it is their fault. It never occurs to them that the Powers on high might hold them responsible for their enemy's misfortunes and that they are preparing a terrible karma for themselves.

Even if you have been cheated or disappointed by someone this does not give you the right to go about telling everyone what he has done. You may say, "But I'm only doing it to set the record straight. It's a question of justice!" This is where you are mistaken. That notion of justice is the source of all your misfortunes. Everybody seems to think he has the right to punish others and teach them a lesson in the name of justice! Leave justice alone. You might ask, "What should I do then?" You should have recourse to a principle which is above justice, a principle of love, kindness and generosity.

It is already two thousand years since Jesus gave us this new doctrine of love and, in spite of it, Christians still apply the law of Moses : an eye for an eye and a tooth for a tooth. They still have not understood that if they want to become truly big and free they will have to stop applying that antiquated notion of justice. Do you think you will feel triumphant if you see your enemy completely ruined? It is more than probable that you will not feel particularly proud of yourself and will begin to be sorry for what you did. But by then it will be too late and you will have prepared very hard times for yourself, in this incarnation or in the next.

You must learn to adopt a totally different attitude. Let's suppose that you have done someone a kindness, lent him some money, for instance, and then, one day, you find that he does not deserve all you have done for him and you go and tell everybody about your generosity and about his supposed unworthiness. Why do you have to talk about it? If you do something good and then go and tell everyone about it, you are undoing all the good you did. It was ordained on high that you would be rewarded but then you go and spoil it all by erasing your good deed.

Even if someone cheats you and does you an injury, it does not matter. Never talk about it. On the contrary, your whole attitude should show that person that you are better than he is. One day he will end by being ashamed of himself and not only will he do everything in his power to right the wrong he did you, but he will take you as his model. When are you going to make up your minds to behave with high-mindedness and generosity? You must learn to close your eyes to some things and to forgive. This is the only way to grow and become a truly noble being. If you learn to do this, even the things you lost will be given back to you a hundred-fold. Otherwise, when you try to revenge yourself, you create so many negative forces that one day they will come back at you and it is you who will be submerged by them. When this happens you will perhaps understand that you behaved like an imbecile! Whatever anyone does to you therefore, never try to get your own back. Wait for Heaven to pass judgment in your favour, for this it will inevitably do if you behave irreproachably.

I think you should begin to realize how very useful it is to receive the light of Initiatic Science. When the average man who knows nothing of this is wronged or annoyed by someone, obviously he responds by teaching him a lesson – so-called – and everyone thinks that that is only normal and just. Well, perhaps it is justice in the eyes of the crowd but as I have already explained, justice as it is understood by the common man is simply stupidity in the eyes of an Initiate. For, look what happens next: since this man has acted on his desire for revenge, he is automatically caught up in a vicious circle from which there is no escape. He has got rid of one enemy: true! But there will always be others to take his place and he will have to try and get rid of them. In other words, he has put himself in the position of having to foster negative feelings and attitudes which can only strengthen his lower nature, and in the end, what will he have gained? Absolutely nothing! For all those enemies he has massacred are going to come back. They have never really ceased to exist. They will reincarnate and one day it will be their turn to revenge themselves. And this is how anyone who thinks he can get rid of his opponents is, in reality, only preparing others for the future and, in the end, it is he who will succumb.

This old method of revenge is no solution. On the contrary, it complicates things, burdens a man's existence and multiplies his karmic debt. In the long run it leads to his downfall and eventual disappearance. No one can pretend that in seeking revenge, man is obeying the dictates of a sublime intelligence!

In contrast, take the case of a true Initiate. He too has been outraged and defiled, trodden under, wronged and humiliated by enemies. But as he knows the law, he responds with other methods.

Instead of revenging himself directly on his adversaries he leaves them strictly alone: they are free to develop in whatever way they want. And, secure in the knowledge of how they will end up, in the meantime, he begins to get ready. What is he getting ready for? To massacre them? No. I have already explained that he refuses to assume a debt towards them, he intends to maintain his freedom and develop his power. And power does not mean getting your gun and shooting your enemy. That is not power, but weakness... and ignorance besides!

An Initiate gets ready in a different way. He says, "Aha, you thought you'd wiped me out, eh? Just you wait. You're in for a surprise!" And he sets to work to pursue a stupendous work of transformation on himself. He prays and meditates, studies and practices until one day, he has acquired true wisdom and true power. And if, when this is done, he meets his old enemies again, they are dumbfounded. Something indescribable begins to happen in their minds and in their hearts and souls. Seeing the light that flows from the Initiate who, instead of wasting his time trying to get even with them, has been working on his own transformation, they feel tarnished and ugly. They begin to realize that they have been wasting their life and they decide to change. And lo and behold, here is the Initiate's true triumph, his true victory: without so much as laying a finger on them, simply by leaving them alone, he has gained the upper hand over his enemies.

In Bulgaria we have a saying, "No need to push a drunkard, he'll fall over by himself." And it is quite true. Someone who is drunk with pride and self-sufficiency, who is intoxicated with his own grandeur, will fall over all by himself one day, without any assistance from you! If you push him, the law will hold you responsible for his fall, but if you leave him alone he will inevitably fall over and it will not be on your conscience. In the meantime, you will have been busy improving yourself, concerned only with things pure, luminous and divine. Is this not by far the best solution? Of course it is! It is a method which demands a great deal of love, kindness, patience and light, but for my part I know of none better. Without ill will, without vindictiveness of any kind, you will heap coals of fire on the heads of your enemies: they will see you and that will be enough for them. They will regret their behaviour and will come and make reparation for the wrong they did you.

For there is after all a natural law, according to which anyone who has done you wrong will be obliged, one day or another, in this life or in a future incarnation, to come and find you and make amends. When this happens, you may feel intuitively that they are old enemies and you may try to keep them at a distance. This will not make any difference. They will keep coming back and insisting that you accept their offers of help. This is the law, and it has already proved true for many of you. Everybody who has ever wronged you and whom you have not wronged in return is obliged by the law to come and make amends to you, whether he likes it or not. His opinion is of no importance.

An Initiate is capable of revenge therefore, but only with the weapons of light and love. And you, too, can revenge yourselves. It is normal to revenge oneself. Why not? But there are two ways of doing it: the first is to knock out your enemy and tear him apart; the second is to leave him intact but to induce a radical change in his heart and soul which can only be beneficial both to him and to you. The second way is twice as good as the first.

I most sincerely advise all the members of the Brotherhood therefore, to do everything in their power to settle their conflicts without creating more karma for themselves. Why is it that even members of the same family have to go to court to settle their disputes over money? When are they going to learn to be above such methods? Why do humans always cling to their interests and their possessions? If they could just make one little gesture, they would find freedom! They might not feel free right away, in fact they might be a bit ill at ease and even suffer from it to begin with, but if they can bring themselves to make a gesture of disin-

terestedness and abnegation they will soon discover
new dimensions, a new light, and none will be
prouder or happier than they, because they will
have achieved something very difficult: a victory
over their lower nature or personality.

It is your personality, your lower self, which is
always urging you on to grab the lion's share, to
take your revenge, to slander others and take them
to court. And with it all you believe you have understood the Teaching! Let me disillusion you.
Those who behave like that have not understood
the first thing about the Teaching. They listen to
the lectures and read the books and exclaim in admiration... and then they go on behaving exactly as
they have always done. Do not think for a moment
that I am blind to all that. It is really pitiful: how
can they go on behaving like everybody else when
they have been privileged to witness so much light,
when so many tremendous truths have been revealed to them?

If you count on divine love, wisdom and generosity to help you solve all your problems you will
never be alone because you will have forged a bond
with Heaven. And here again is a point that many
of you have still not understood. You still do not
really believe and trust sufficiently in the power of
the hidden world to sustain you and smooth out
your path if you work in their way. You are always
only too ready to trust in all the intrigues and de-

ceits suggested by your personalities. And this is why you never really succeed in any of your enterprises : sooner or later the invisible world bars your way. Whereas Initiates and those who respect the laws and count on Heaven to help them are never abandoned, even if the whole world forsakes them, they are sustained, encouraged and enlightened and in the long run, they always triumph.

III

So you intend to revenge yourself on someone who has done you an injury, is that it? Very well. For the sake of argument, let's say that you are entitled to do so, but let me ask you one thing: do you know for certain exactly what punishment he deserves? Perhaps you will say, "Yes. It's perfectly simple: he hit me and I'm going to hit him back!" All right, but you had better think again. Can you give him *exactly* what he gave you? Of course you cannot. And all the more so if the injury he did you is not so simple: you can never do exactly as much harm to someone as he has done to you. It is far better not to get involved. Leave it to those who are capable of paying each creature his just deserts. If not, in your ignorance you will only go and make some silly mistake which you will have to pay for later: in the future, you will meet this same enemy again and your problems with him will begin all over again.

This fact of the impossibility of rendering absolute justice is illustrated in a very original way by

Shakespeare in *The Merchant of Venice.* The money-lender, Shylock, had lent Antonio, the merchant, three thousand ducats with the agreement that if the money was not repaid by a certain date he would have the right to cut a pound of flesh off Antonio's body. When the fatal day arrived, Antonio could not pay because his ship had sunk at sea taking with it his entire fortune, so Shylock took him to court charging him with not honouring his contract, and claimed his pound of flesh. Since no plea for pity could make Shylock renounce his claim, the judge reluctantly ordered Antonio to pay his debt. But then one of the judges (who was really a young woman in disguise), intervened, calling for scales to be brought. Then, telling Antonio to bare his breast, he told Shylock to take his pound of flesh, but without spilling any blood, for the contract specified only flesh. If Shylock spilled so much as one drop of blood, warned the judge, his fortune would be confiscated. Of course, Shylock was very alarmed and tried to withdraw the charge. But the judge insisted and this time he added, "If thou tak'st more or less than a just pound... nay, if the scale do turn but in the estimation of a hair, thou diest and all thy goods are confiscate." Shylock was even more panic-stricken. Finally all ended well, thanks to the wisdom of this young woman who understood how imperfect human justice was.

Even if one could calculate the exact punishment due, to be truly just one would also have to
make sure that the circumstances were the same.
Does a fine of £100 for instance, really represent
the same degree of punishment to someone who
has only that to live on, as to a multi-millionaire?
Of course not. So, you see, it is virtually impossible
to do justice. And this is why, if you think that
someone who has wronged you fully deserves to be
punished, you should speak to the invisible world
about it. "You see, this person did thus and so to
me and, because of that, I'm having all kinds of difficulties in such and such a way. So I'm asking you
to intervene and right this wrong." In this way you
lodge your complaint with the heavenly courts of
justice in exactly the same way as one does in
everyday life on earth; Heaven will judge the case
and decide what to do about it. Whatever happens,
be sure not to do anything yourself.

The reason why you must do nothing is that
there is an element here which you simply cannot
know, and that is that certain unpleasant events occur in your life for certain very specific reasons. It
could be that the person you are complaining
about was guided in his actions by the invisible
world in order to teach you something, so that you
would understand some particular truth or even to
force you to make more rapid progress. And that
being so, why not use these circumstances as an oc-

casion to work on yourself and accomplish real progress instead of ruminating all kinds of ideas of revenge, rebelling against Heaven because your enemy has not been exterminated, or taking revenge on other innocent people, as so often happens in life?

You must learn therefore to behave correctly even if others behave very badly towards you. It is not your business to punish them. There are laws in the universe which will take care of that. As for you, you must avoid entertaining negative ideas because they will have a very detrimental effect on your psychic health and one day your face will reflect all the bad feelings you have nourished. You may say that you are only defending your rights... perhaps. But you are still working against your own best interests and, if you persist, you will never get on to the right road.

5

THE LAW OF CORRESPONDENCES

I

The human organism is a microcosm, an exact replica of the universe, or macrocosm. Hence, between man and the universe there are points and zones which correspond and the whole of esoteric science is based on this law of correspondences. Man is infinitely small, the cosmos is infinitely vast, but between the infinitely small and the infinitely vast there is correspondence: each organ of the human body has an affinity with a given region of the cosmos. Of course, you must not think that I am saying that the cosmos has organs like ours, but in essence, our organs and those of the cosmos have something identical in common. Thanks to the law of affinity we can establish contact with forces, centres and worlds in space which correspond to certain elements within us. A knowledge of these correspondences can open up unheard-of possibilities for us.

Between man, the microcosm and the universe, the macrocosm, an absolute correspondence exists.

But, since man has destroyed his original ideal relationship with the macrocosm and with God by his disordered way of life, the problem now is to restore that bond. And this is within our reach, for when man was first created, he was endowed with all he needed to advance and develop and, in case he got lost, to find his way back to his heavenly homeland.

When a child comes into this world he has everything he needs: his heart may be a touch too far to the right, his stomach rather small or his kidneys may not function perfectly, but at least he has a heart, a stomach, kidneys, lungs, etc. Nothing is missing. In exactly the same way, every spirit which incarnates on this earth possesses organs and faculties which correspond to all the virtues and qualities on high in Heaven, and this being so, everything is possible to him. Not all at once, of course, but gradually, if he knows and abides by the laws, he can undertake the most stupendous tasks.

What are the laws in question? Well, suppose you have two tuning forks: if you set one of them vibrating you will find that the other one vibrates also, without your having touched it. This is what is known as resonance. Everybody knows about this phenomenon but no one stops to analyse it and to see that exactly the same thing occurs between a human being and the cosmos. If a man tunes his physical and psychological being to the same vibrations as those of the universe, he can reach out to touch the heavenly powers and establish a bond and an interaction with them which will help and comfort him. Vibrations are a means of communication. You speak and someone hears you. You can even set certain forces in motion so that they can reach you and you can benefit from them. There is interaction, therefore, between you and any region of the universe you choose, and you must know that it is precisely in this interaction that God has placed man's very best means to attain perfection.

You will ask, "How can we attune ourselves? It's all very complicated." No, don't worry, it will happen all by itself. If you cultivate love, selflessness, indulgence and generosity, your whole being will begin to be attuned, because you will be working with forces which automatically bring everything into harmony within you. When someone ruins his nervous system, does he do it consciously, scientifically and in all lucidity? Does he know exactly where and to what extent he is creating havoc? No, of course not! But because he entertained all kinds of outlandish thoughts and feelings, he ended by breaking down. It is not necessary to know exactly where all your nerve centres are to go out of your mind! And it is the same if you want to attune your whole being: you simply have to enter-

tain elevated thoughts and feelings and they will set
your spiritual centres vibrating harmoniously.

Some people who have done everything possible to ensure that nothing functions properly, are
always complaining that life is meaningless and
that God does not exist. But the fact that they are
stupid, ill and unhappy does not mean that nobody
in the whole wide world is intelligent, happy and in
good health. It is only their reasoning that is at
fault. If they corrected that, everything else would
improve too. And suppose that it is you who are
unhappy and anxious, nothing goes right for you,
what should you do? Instead of standing there
wringing your hands and weeping, why not go and
find someone who could help you? "Where are
they and how can I find them?" you ask. They are
right beside you all the time, you have only to
think about them to reach them, thanks to the law
of resonance or, as I like to call it, the law of affinity. As soon as you know this law you are in possession of the means of rising above yourself and
reaching out beyond your limitations to touch the
most subtle and sensitive cords of your being and
set them throbbing, knowing that there are corresponding forces, entities and regions in space which
will respond.

The acoustical law of resonance, the phenomenon of the echo, first made me stop and think. You

call out, "I love you" and even if you are alone a whole host of voices reply, "I love you, I love you, I love you." If you call out "I hate you," the echo sends it back to you too. And since this happens on the physical plane, why should it not happen on the mental plane also?

Or take a ball and throw it against the wall: if you forget to step aside it will bounce back and hit you. Basically the ball is obeying the same law as your voice: the boomerang effect. Here too, everyone knows this law on the physical plane but nobody believes that it applies equally on the psychological and spiritual planes. Whatever you do, good or evil, will necessarily come back to you one day. Every feeling you experience falls into a certain category and it goes out into space, awakening kindred forces which then come back to you, according to the law of affinity. And it is thanks to this law that man can draw on the immense reservoirs of the universe and obtain all the elements he wants, just as long as he projects into space thoughts and feelings of the same breed as those he wants to attract to himself. It is the nature of your own thoughts and feelings which exactly and unfailingly determines which forces and elements you awaken and attract to yourself from outer space.

To my mind this law of affinity is the most important key, the great Arcanum, the magic wand. My whole life has been based on it. Knowing the law I can orient all my work in a certain direction, thinking of all that is the most beautiful, the best for me, and then I wait for the results. Many of the things I have worked for have already come about; others will come later. I do not need to apply any other law for this one includes them all, thanks to it I can explain everything to you: how human beings are constructed, their intelligence and their stupidity, their kindness and their hard-heartedness, their misfortunes and their happiness, their wealth and their poverty... everything!

Look at what happens with fish in the ocean. The ocean contains an infinite variety of chemical elements, and one kind of fish, simply because it attracts certain elements and particles, fashions for itself a magnificent, colourful, phosphorescent body, whereas another attracts different particles and its body is dingy and ugly. Of course it is not a conscious process, but the fact remains: each fish draws from the sea those elements which correspond to its nature. This applies to us, too. We are little fish immersed in the waters of the etheric ocean and, as that ocean contains all the elements provided by the Creator, we become thus and so thanks to the particular elements we have drawn from the ocean to form our bodies. Everything can be explained by this. Take the case of someone who is ugly, unhappy and always ill: his troubles do not come from his present incarnation but from previous ones, when he was neither instructed nor guided, and when, in his ignorance, he attracted to himself all kinds of objectionable elements, and now he does not know how to get rid of them.

So be careful. You who know this law of affinity, the most potent law of magic and the foundation of the whole of creation, you must immediately set to work to attract to yourself particles of so luminous a nature that you will begin to get better in every way. And when those you live and work with see that you have become much more friendly and radiant, that you even seem to be more intelligent and, above all, stronger and more forceful, they will begin to have a better opinion of you and your destiny will change. You see, everything in life is connected. Whereas if you are ignorant, if you do not know the laws on which all creation is based and if you are forever tearing down and destroying all that God has given you, then of course, the forces of nature cannot help you for long. In the end they are obliged to leave you to your own resources. And then what sorrow and heartbreak follow!

Unfortunately, a great many men and women are in this state. I have met so many of them. They had no idea of how they had got into such a sorry state and their minds were in such chaos and obscurity I could not even explain it to them: they could see no point to life, no order in the universe –

nothing! I would have had to start from the very beginning and instruct them for years on end and, above all, it would have taken willpower, they would have had to be stimulated by the will to listen and to learn. They did not have this will and it was impossible to explain to them in five minutes the whole sequence of events that had brought them to their present plight: where and when they had begun to go astray and how, little by little, they had brought it on themselves. Unfortunately most people refuse to recognize this sequence of cause and effect in their lives even if one demonstrates it with almost tangible arguments and proofs.

To my mind, then, the word "affinity" is one of the most significant words that exists: it is a magic word. For it is this law of affinity which makes it possible for us to draw from the waters of the cosmic ocean the best elements, the most radiant and subtle elements with which to build our body of glory. I have already talked to you about this body of glory, or Body of Light as it is sometimes called, the immortal spark hidden in the innermost being of each man and woman. The Gospels mention it, but give no details. As I have explained in other lectures, we all have a potential body of glory within us, but we have to form it by giving it the materials it needs in order to grow, just as the mother does for the child in her womb.

How does a mother form her baby? By everything she eats, drinks, breathes or thinks, simply by living, she gives it the materials it needs to grow and develop. It is she who forms her child and she cannot do more than that. She cannot create it. Nor can we create Christ in us: our souls must be impregnated with the divine seed before Christ can be conceived in us. Only then, like a human mother, can we nourish and form him with everything that emanates from us, with all that is pure and good in our lives.

When, from time to time, we experience a really elevated state of consciousness, when we have the desire to help the entire world, to work only for the Lord, to deny ourselves and do something really lofty and noble, then the particles that emanate from us go to nourish and strengthen our body of glory. This is the only way we can make it grow: it can be formed only by the very best in us. And if we nourish it over long years with our flesh and blood, with our fluids and our very lives, one day it will become radiant and glowing with light. One day it will become strong, potent and invulnerable to attack. One day it will be immortal, made of immortal materials, impervious to wear or corrosion. And when this day comes, this body of glory will work wonders within us and around us and Christ himself will be able to use it to accomplish miracles.

Until he has formed this inner body, man remains insignificant, obscure, weak, vulnerable and
sickly, and yet every human being carries within
him the seed of Christ, waiting to be developed.
And this brings us back to the law of affinity. The
disciple must surpass himself, rise above himself in
order to attract the purest and most luminous particles from the ocean of etheric waters and fuse
them to his body of glory. He can begin to attract a
few straight away, today, and gradually, each day,
he will attract more and more. In fact, that is what
we do every morning when we go to the sunrise:
detaching ourselves more and more from the earth,
we link up with Heaven, with the sun itself, and
glean some particles of light to add to our body of
glory. All this is a fragment from the book of true
Knowledge.

For years and years I worked with only one idea
in mind: to know and understand the structure of
that marvellous edifice, the universe. For years it
was my only interest and I spent days and nights
out of my body seeking a clear view of that frame-
work and the links which connect all the different
elements of the universe. I knew that nothing else
mattered. The only thing that really matters, that is
really essential, is to see the over-all structure, and
this is why, as long as man is content to study the
disparate elements of the physical world, the world

of facts, he will reach only false conclusions. Only by rising to the higher plane of the laws and even higher still to the level of principles, will he reach a vantage point from which he will have the clear view of the whole that I obtained. It took me years, but now I have it, and that is why today I can instruct and enlighten you and give you advice: because my frame of reference is always the cosmic model of perfection.

No one, or hardly anyone, recognizes the true value of this philosophy yet. But this will not always be so. There are forces more powerful than men at work in the universe and they will one day oblige men to arrive at an appreciation of the true worth of the Teaching. I am absolutely sure of this and that is why I never worry. I live in the conviction that, sooner or later, everything will fall into place.

For the moment, everything on earth is upside down: anything of real value is scoffed at while things that have no value at all are given first place. See for yourself: people attach enormous importance to gold, jewelry, houses and cars, whereas ideas from Heaven are ridiculed and scorned. This is the exact opposite of the order observed in the structure of the cosmos: above all else, in the highest place, is an idea, a truth. That is what has preeminence in the world above: an idea. Everything else is subservient to that.

Human beings have reversed all the values: nothing is in its rightful place anymore. You can see the most vicious and diabolical people surrounded by wealth and splendour, whereas those who possess the very highest qualities have none of the corresponding exterior trappings. As they are bereft of acquisitiveness they do nothing to obtain worldly riches and so they possess only the strict minimum on the physical plane. Exteriorly, nothing can be seen of all their inner splendour. But this state of affairs will not last forever because the law of correspondences demands that inner beauty be clothed in outer beauty and that inner ugliness be clothed in outer ugliness. The Intelligence of nature has decreed that it should be so.

In the distant past, when the true order of things was respected, all those who were interiorly indigent were exteriorly poor, too, and those who had great interior wealth also enjoyed exterior wealth. Just like the Lord Himself! God, who possesses all qualities and virtues, also possesses the whole universe. It is only here in human society that this order is not respected, but as the law is absolute ("As above, so below"), things will be ordained differently one day, and everyone will regain his rightful place: those who are rich in intelligence, kindness and nobleness, will be endowed with corresponding exterior riches and those who have none of these inner qualities will be poverty-stricken. Obviously it is not human beings who are going to restore the right order, for they have no notion of who is meritorious and who is not. It will be done by Cosmic Intelligence, for the law of correspondences is an immutable law of the universe.

What I have given you today is a key: the key to the mastery of your own destiny. Use your thoughts and feelings to produce much more elevated vibrations and emanations which will spontaneously seek out kindred elements from among all those billions which exist in cosmic space. If you do this you will, once again, gain control of your own destiny.

II

The law of correspondences is a physical, chemical, magical and spiritual law which can be expressed in these words: when someone tunes in to what is perfect – be it perfection of intelligence, power, form, colour, perfume or beauty – he benefits from that perfection because he introduces it into his own being. This is an infallible law, and from the first moment that you know it, you can no longer rid yourself of the idea of perfection without feeling that you are destroying something in yourself. This law is the basis and foundation of all true religion. Why is man told to love God? Because by loving Him and meditating on Him he forms a bond with His perfection and splendour and then that divine splendour begins to take up its abode within him and it is he who grows and blossoms, who becomes beautiful and powerful.

If you fail to respect this law, no one in Heaven or earth can help you. Before you knew about it, who helped you? The Lord? Certainly not. He

may not even have known what you were up to!
But as soon as you do anything that touches this
law, you set in motion a process of aid and encour-
agement that eventually frees you from all your difficulty and suffering. If, in spite of all your love for
God you have not yet reached this point of freedom, it is because you built up such a heavy layer
of armour around yourself in previous incarnations
that even though you may now be working in harmony with this law and even if it is already accu-
mulating tremendous treasures within you, you
cannot feel them. But persevere! Little by little
your defensive shell will wear away and will end by
disappearing altogether. When this day comes, all
that you have stored up through your thoughts,
prayers and contemplation, all that wealth, all
those treasures, all that beauty and splendour, will
pour forth and inundate you. Without realizing it
you will have accumulated an ocean of blessings
which is there around you, just waiting to inundate
you!

If your religion is founded only on beliefs or
customs instilled in you by your education or your
environment, it cannot be very strong or durable.
True religion is founded on a knowledge of the law
of affinity. When you know this law, then you
know that you must love God and think about
Him, not because the Church tells you to or be-

cause it says so in the Bible, but because there is an
absolute law which says that the true beneficiary of
that love is yourself, and, through you the whole
world. But this knowledge has not yet penetrated
into our heads : the fact that so many Christians are
leaving the Church these days is proof enough of
this. Religion as they understood it has no solid
foundation. What they need, now, is Initiatic
knowledge, the Secret Knowledge of the Mysteries
revealed in the ancient Initiations. A disciple who
was guided by his master through certain experi-
ences had a physical knowledge of reality and
could never again doubt what he had learned in
this way. It was knowledge that had as it were become part of his own flesh and nothing could take
it away from him.

The closer you come to God, the happier you
will be and the more you will live in power, omni-
science and eternity, because you are attracting to
yourself all the particles, forces, rays, currents –
call them what you like – which come from Him.
Never take counsel from the ignorant, from all
those who make pronouncements about the Lord
with complete assurance – especially when they de-
clare that he does not exist! What do they know
that entitles them to lay down the law? What I am
telling you here today has been verified for thousands of years. I too have verified it and continue to
do so every moment of the day.

God has no need of our love, of our gratitude, of our prayers. It is we who need to love Him and to pray to Him. Some people decide not to go to Church anymore, not to light any more candles to Him, as a punishment! He has failed to serve their interests, so He must be punished. Oh! goodness, what weeping and lamentation, how He tears His hair, the poor Lord, all because He has been dropped by some idiot! This is the mentality of a lot of human beings. I repeat, it is to man's interest to believe in God and to pray to Him. If you refuse God, you must realize that you will inevitably put other gods in His place and, as they will have none of His perfection, you will develop their vices, weakness and illness yourself. Go ahead, turn your back on Him if you want to. He is so far above us He will not even notice. He has stopped up His ears to the chatter of human beings, but they will be the ones to suffer, because they are depriving themselves of all His splendours.

Nations and societies which have decided to do away with God are, whether they realize it or not, disintegrating. For the time being they feel secure, protected from all ill effects, but one day they will appreciate what they lost. Like the man who made a pact with the Devil to keep him supplied with money. The Devil agreed, "All right, but every time I bring you money you will give me a hair of your head in exchange." "Oh," said the man, "that's nothing. A hair...." Yes, but in no time at all he was bald! This brought about all kinds of changes in his life. A lot of people reason, "What can you possibly lose by severing your bonds with God and doing what you like? Nothing happens." They are wrong, something does happen: every time you do something wrong you lose a tiny particle of vitality, freshness and charm, and in the end, even if you have gained materially, you will have lost your most precious assets.

I insist, do not let a single day go by without linking up with Heaven for, in this way, thanks to the law of affinity, you will trigger all kinds of processes which will have important repercussions. To my mind it is the most stupid thing anyone can do, to cut oneself off from the Heavenly Father. There are all kinds of stupid things one can do – I hardly need to enumerate them for you, but the worst and most stupid of all is that, because it leads to all the others. I am not asking anyone to become a religious fanatic, like the people who are always in Church lighting candles and reciting their prayers with forbidding expressions on their faces. If they were sincere about their religion they would long ago have changed and acquired radiance and beauty. But no, they never get any better, and this shows that their religion is still an exterior practice. Everyone has not the same notion of religion!

Nowadays religion is not held in as great esteem as in the past when religion, priests and the Church were universally respected. Many priests sense this change of attitude, and try to keep contact with the masses by organizing all kinds of popular activities in their Churches. You see them there in the crowd: chubby, red-faced and jovial... truly priest-ly figures! Nothing is sacred in church anymore: bingo, folk-music, discussions, dances.... The clergy is at a loss to know what to think up next to attract the crowd. All this is completely off the mark. The only thing that can save the Church throughout the world is the Initiatic Science, be-cause it is the only solid foundation for religion.

A great many people stop praying, thinking, "It doesn't pay. When you've got a job of work waiting to be done, why go off and pray and meditate? It's a waste of time." Obviously, prayer will not help you with material advantages: money, houses, cars, a high-ranking job, a rich wife. But it brings other advantages: your thoughts put you into con-tact with God, and you receive all kinds of spiritual gifts, force and light. These advantages are invisible but as the invisible side of things is nonetheless real, what you receive has its effect on you and everyone with whom you come in contact. People feel vivified, comforted and consoled, they begin to trust you and offer you all kinds of opportunity, including material advantages. But it all starts with the spiritual side of things.

Material gains should not be expected from your prayer, from your love of God. Many people say, "I pray and pray, but where does it get me? I'm still poor." Obviously, they had hoped to acquire wealth! It is amazing, the distorted understanding they have! Humans need to learn about the realities and laws of the hidden world if they are ever going to understand what true science, true religion and true life are all about. For the moment there is a great deal of misunderstanding: they persist in looking for all sorts of advantages and are totally unaware that in the meantime they are receiving nothing but disadvantages.

When you are tuned in to the Lord you attract to yourself His qualities. They seep into you, penetrating your being and making you a radiant, intelligent and well-balanced human being. When this happens, you may even receive material wealth if such is your destiny, but if the first thing you ask for is material wealth, it shows that you still have not understood. To begin with, you will not necessarily have an easy time, but the invisible side of things will soon begin to improve and even if you cannot see this, you can feel it. Do you never have the feeling that a certain person simply by his presence has a calming effect, he makes you feel at peace, you feel that you are a better human being when you are with him, whereas another always seems to arouse the worst in you? These are invisible phenomena, but they are no less real.

True religion is based on a knowledge of the law of correspondences. As soon as you plug in to a given source, a power-house or a radio-transmitter, you inevitably start receiving particles from that source. And if you tune in to a different transmitter that sends out messages in direct contradiction to the first, you receive them, too. You cannot see them? No matter, one day you will. Today I am giving you some pearls from the treasure-house of true knowledge, known in the past only to the great Initiates. If you welcome them into yourself you will become invincible.

If someone says, "I put the Teaching into practice. I do everything you say to do, and look at me! I feel unbalanced, neurotic, I think that I'm going out of my mind," I can only reply, "you're mistaken in thinking that you're putting the Teaching into practice. There must be something inside you to which you are still giving free rein: pride, or some disorder in your sexual life, an undisciplined imagination, or perhaps you're trying to force the pace and achieve great spiritual results much too quickly? None of this is in keeping with the Teaching, it is not to blame. It could be that you're not going about it the right way. Look for the cause in yourself." The Teaching is there precisely to make people well-balanced, to make them strong and happy, not to destroy them. So, if things are not all well with you, try and find the cause, the law you have broken or the area in which you have been over-indulgent, which has put you in your present sorry state.

Another person says, "I don't want to be with my family anymore. They're not very highly evolved and not at all mystical. I want to free myself from them completely." There again I must answer, "Isn't your reasoning a bit excessive and dangerous? You have bonds that tie you to your family and you can't cut those bonds so easily." In your reasoning, your decisions, your feelings, if you are too personal, it will always produce some anomaly in you. Therefore, if you suffer from all kinds of ailments and infirmities, look for the cause in yourself and your own behaviour, not in the Teaching.

Let other people believe what they like, but you who are being taught the great laws of life, know that you have an obligation to aim for nobility and perfection. All those who reject religion, thinking that what counts is to work for society no matter whether you believe in God or not, are on the wrong road, because in the long run, a society without God degenerates. Without an axis on which to turn, it falls apart, and they themselves will cease to be irreproachable social beings: cupidity, partiality or injustice will inevitably creep in. This is why societies, empires and kingdoms end by disintegrating: they have no stable central point to cling to, to prevent the development of negative forces.

A society that is sound and truly centred on something superior, a sublime, divine ideal, is vibrant with currents of such force that whatever the savage beasts within, they are made powerless. Cowed, they dare not show themselves anymore, and the way is open to establish just laws and build a society of peace and abundance for all. But when the intensity of the spiritual life begins to wane, when the centre or the head is missing, then negative forces come to the surface once again and take possession of individuals, for there is nothing to keep them at bay. If such suffering and misfortune have overtaken humanity in our day, it is because human beings have allowed all the divine, beneficial forces within themselves and within society to become less and less potent.

This, therefore, is the life of a disciple: it turns on the axis of a central idea, and that idea begins by instilling fear and caution into the enemy within. An example on the level of physical health: people who live very disordered lives end by ruining their health and begin to be ravaged by tuberculosis, for

instance. The doctors tell them to lead a more reg-
ular life: less emotion, excitement and passion, a
healthier diet and adequate sleep. If they follow
this treatment, their bodies secrete a certain sub-
stance, antibodies which counteract and paralyse
the bacilli and their health improves. Should the
patient resume his old life, drinking and smoking
and spending his nights in folly, all his defences
crumble and disease once again gets the upper
hand.

Exactly the same law prevails on the psychological level. The life of the spirit helps us to build defences against the forces of evil and to muster our
workers and assistants – for there is a veritable factory in every human being – but if we become care-
less and stop living harmoniously, the forces of im-
balance and darkness assert themselves and mul-
tiply, and we deteriorate. Our best protection is
God Himself, we must bind ourselves to Him so
that the forces He awakens within us become
strong enough to ward off the evil entities which
are always ready to do us harm. If we want to sever
this bond we are perfectly free to do so but sooner
or later, that freedom will cost us very dearly.

These things that I have explained to you today
are a lesson from the book of true Knowledge
which I have studied all my life, not in printed
books, but in my own innermost being. I have immersed myself completely in this study and now it

has become absolutely clear for me. And you too, whatever philosophy may be in fashion at the moment, and whatever people say to you, cling to the idea of a Divinity, seek it, love it, call upon it. This is the only way to receive the potent energies which will prevent your inner enemies from harming you. You may get bitten from time to time if your defences are not absolutely impenetrable, but little by little you will strengthen them and evil will no longer be able to reach you. Christians sing, "The Lord is my Shepherd," but to most of them these are just words, they say them mechanically, knowing nothing of the extraordinary science and magic power hidden in the words.

Believe me, nothing is more important for man than to love his Creator. Nothing is comparable. Because of this love everything falls into place, problems resolve themselves, life becomes harmonious and, even if we fail to get visible results in this incarnation, it does not matter, for entities from on high watch over us and when they see that we are making an intelligent effort, they send us their approval in the form of untold blessings.

6

THE LAWS OF NATURE
AND MORAL LAW

If you observe the behaviour of human beings it soon becomes obvious that they lack a sense of proportion both in the choices they make and in their behaviour in general. Either they never stop stuffing themselves or they eat too little; in either case they undermine their health. Either they work too hard and exhaust themselves or they never do a hand's turn and get completely rusty. And the same is true for feelings and thoughts. To explain such anomalies people say that someone has "overstepped the bounds," that he has broken certain laws which he should have known and respected.

There are certain physical laws which govern nature and our bodies. Human beings may not always obey them but at least they acknowledge their existence. Unfortunately this is not true when it comes to moral laws. Those who acknowledge the existence of moral laws are few and far between nowadays, and even if people still have some faint

belief in the importance of a certain order, most
writers, philosophers, artists and scholars expose
theories, write books and create works whose sole
aim is to dispel the last remnants of this belief. But
it is precisely the moral laws which I want to talk
about today, because when these laws are not rec-
ognized, something essential is missing from human knowledge.

The realm of moral law is not divorced from the
physical world. You can see that for yourself in the
case of a drunkard, for instance. To begin with he
is kind and thoughtful, pleasant, cultured, honest
and generous – he has all the virtues! But as he begins to drink, these virtues fade away and before
long they disappear without a trace. Or take another case: a man has such a passion for gambling
that he ends by neglecting his duty and forgetting
his wife and children and his job. To begin with,
his gambling is an activity with no moral connota-
tions, but in the end, it is the moral dimension of
the man that suffers. How is it that humans fail to
see the connection between the two worlds? They
believe only in the value of the physical, material
world. That is all well and good, it is very important. But the moral dimension, the inner, ethical
dimension is very closely linked to it.

According to Initiatic Science there are three
worlds: the divine world which is the level of ideas,
the psychic world which is the level of thoughts

and feelings (it is on this level that we find the moral laws) and finally the physical world, the world of forms and materialization. The material world is linked to the moral world which in turn is linked to the far higher world of ideas. If human beings cannot see these connections it is because they have failed to study and observe what surrounds them, and until they do so they will suffer the disastrous effects of their own ignorance.

Ignorance is no defence before the law: even if you do not know the moral laws, if you flout them by your behaviour, you will be obliged to suffer the consequences. When this happens, perhaps you will begin to notice that they exist and that they are much subtler than those of the physical world, because they are not written into the physical body alone, but into man's soul and spirit as well. Those who do not abide by them are labelled self-centred egoists by others and, before long, they begin to feel deprived of support and friendship. Whatever the offence they will have to pay for it. In what currency? This can vary a great deal: it can be remorse, pain or suffering, bitterness, regret and disappointment, sometimes money. You can notice this on all levels.

Everything is linked. The moral domain is governed by immutable, indestructible laws which you should know. They are often ignored because they are not written down anywhere and people think they have the right to do whatever they please. This is not so: until such time as people realize that these laws exist they will never make any real progress. It is unacceptable to go only by your own rules of conduct, you cannot say, "I can do what I please!" Why not? Because you will pay for it if you do. You think you have every right to do thus and so... all right. Do as you please but know that you will pay for it. In the natural order everything has to be paid for, even happiness and joy, even ecstasy. "But I haven't any money." These laws will not ask for your money (only human beings ask for money), but they will ask you to pay with some of your strength, some of your knowledge, health or beauty, some of your inner light. If you manage to analyse yourself you will see that your books do not balance: the bailiffs have been! That is, Cosmic Forces, the intelligent beings who govern the universe, have visited you and taken away something and you are that much the poorer!

If you want to become very rich you must disobey neither the laws of nature, nor moral laws, nor human laws. Although man-made laws are not of the same kind as the natural laws, as long as one lives in a society in which they still prevail it is preferable to obey them (to respect the Highway Code, for instance). If you break man-made laws without being found out, nature will not hold it against you, it is not her concern. But if you break

one of nature's laws, even if society continues to respect and honour you, you will fall ill. Yes, the
natural law will put you to bed! Nature will punish
you and, go where you will, you cannot escape,
wherever you go, the law will catch up with you
because your record is filed in your own innermost
being.

Nature knew in advance that men would always
manage to break her laws so she put miniature
tape-recorders into them. And now all she has to
do is to glance into us and she can see exactly what
we have eaten and drunk, what we have thought,
felt or done. Quite impossible to cheat! And you
think you can convince me that only human beings
make recordings? How could men make anything
at all if nature did not give them the idea in the first
place? Nature recorded things long before man,
but man is too blind to see this. So, nature has tak-
en the necessary precautions, and if man breaks her
laws he has to pay.

From now on, therefore, try not to break any
laws whether man-made or natural, and especially,
try not to break the moral laws which are superior
to the natural laws. In point of fact, of course, moral laws are part of nature, for nature includes different degrees or levels. On the lowest level is the
purely physical nature. Above that is a more subtle
nature which is the level of thoughts and feelings.
And the last degree, which is above both of these, is

the level of the divine world. Nature too obeys the laws of her highest degree. Just as we have to obey nature's laws, nature obeys the laws of the spirit, for the spirit commands nature. When a man has reached the stage where he can rise above the first two levels: his physical nature and his more subtle nature of thoughts and feelings, he is beyond the reach of laws. He is then so pure, in such perfect harmony with the spirit, and he disposes of such tremendous powers, that even nature obeys him, and whatever he does he never breaks a law. Only when he has reached this state can man do exactly as he pleases without there being any danger of his breaking the law.

Only very exceptional beings, those who are predestined to do so, manage to rise above the natural and moral laws. Such beings have always existed, they exist today and they will continue to exist – but they are very rare. They can do whatever they like without ever committing a crime or a sin. I have had some fantastic revelations on this subject but it is very difficult to explain, it is even impossible to give you even the faintest idea, because it cannot be put into words.

However, I will try to say something to help you to understand. If a man is very pure and radiates light, whatever he does will always be right. If a man is filthy and full of darkness, if he lives in the nether world, even if he decides to do a good deed, he always soils whatever he touches. He is like a man whose hands are black with dirt and grease and who tries to wipe a little speck of dust off his friend's face: he only succeeds in making it dirtier. In his desire to purify others, such a man sullies them; in trying to simplify their lives all he does is complicate them. And why is this? Because everything emanating from him is so chaotic and vile that whatever he does is always destructive. But if a being is pure light, pure love, pure intelligence, even if he strikes someone, instead of killing, the blow saves, because everything in that man and everything that emanates from him is divine. To reach this peak, to dwell in the Sephira Kether, one must have been predestined by the Twenty-four Elders way back in the past. As long as a disciple is still on the road, he must understand that there are laws that he is bound to respect.

Human beings readily admit that in their professional work certain types of behaviour are acceptable and others are not, but when it comes to morality, they think there are no rules. This is where they are highly mistaken. When Hermes Trismegistus said, "As above, so below," he was proclaiming this fact without going into detail, and his words apply to all levels, all areas, all human activities. A tremendous number of activities, objects, colours, forms, beings and regions are included in these two words: "above" and "below."

A lot of people have understood the dictum to mean that what is below, that is, on earth, is similar to what is in Heaven. But this is not true : what is on earth is not like what is in Heaven, the forms and dimensions, the light and the colours, the glory and the splendour are not the same on earth as in Heaven. It is the laws that are the same. Hermes did not specify this because he wanted his words to convey a far vaster meaning, which only those who were capable of entering into the point of view of a great thinker or Initiate would be able to understand.

Thanks to their understanding of the laws which govern the physical world, scientists can boast of amazing achievements, such as the expeditions to the moon, for instance. If they understood the moral laws, their achievements would be greater still, and not only on the material level but also in the vast, infinite realm of the soul and the spirit. They are well versed in physics and chemistry, but there is a spiritual physics, there is a spiritual chemistry they know nothing about. An essential element is missing, therefore, in official science, which is a knowledge of the psychic world governed by moral laws. And since, in addition, today's intellectuals do all they can to erase the last traces of moral sense from human consciences, they are working for the destruction of humanity. Everything will fall apart because of those who deny the existence of moral laws and refuse to abide by them.

It is not always easy to identify these laws, but that is no reason to claim that they do not exist. Nothing can justify you in belittling or denying what I have just said. If you are capable of observation and analysis and if you have enough patience, sooner or later it will become evident to you that every inner transgression of the law has to be paid for, because our inner world is governed by the immortal precepts of eternal law.

You commit a breach of the law and you say, "I'm still eating and drinking, I sleep well, I'm still earning money and my health is fine: nothing is changed." Very well, all that this means is that you are blind! You cannot see what is happening on the subtler levels of your being. You may go on like that for years, trafficking and conniving without ever noticing that every time you do something dishonest you lose something. And what is that "something"? You will have to find that out for yourself. What I can tell you is that I know in advance what you will lose and what tremendous and fearful changes will take place in your innermost being. In a few years you will have lost all your freshness, all your impetus and above all, everything in life will have become utterly tasteless to you. These are immense losses from the spiritual point of view, and if you cannot see this it is be-

cause you are still on a level with the animals! It
may very well be that you go on working and making a lot of money, but you will not be a son or a
daughter of God, supple, alive and radiant with
light. Deep inside you some very big changes take
place.

Animals eat, hunt, fight and caress each other
and protect their young; a great many human beings do no more than that. They do not know that
they have been sent to this earth with a mission: to
manifest the glory of God and to bring to full flow-
ering all that is subtle and divine in their nature.
They have been sent to turn the earth into a Garden of Eden. That is their mission, but they have
forgotten it. They eat and drink and put down roots
in the world and have no desire ever to detach
themselves from it. So then they are uprooted and
packed off upstairs where they learn that they have
wasted their lives and then, obviously, they suffer:
Purgatory and Hell are nothing else. When they
have paid and been made clean they move up still
higher to the first Heaven and then, once again,
they come back to earth in order to continue their
evolution towards perfection. This is the story of
the human race.

Men need to be constantly reminded of their
mission on earth, "What are you here for? Try and
remember!" Remember? How can one remem-

ber? In an Initiatic School, with the help of the
great truths he learns and all the beneficial influences he receives, with the help of the angels, the
disciple begins to remember the world of light he
came from and to which one day he will return.
The greatest blessing a disciple can receive is to remember. He will remember all he has suffered and
the faults he has committed as well as the debts he
owes. He needs to know all this so that he can go
and find those he has wronged in the past, make his
peace with them and atone for his faults, thereby
paying off his karmic debt. This is what is in store
for the disciple – for each one of you. One day you
will be obliged to pay for all that you have taken
dishonestly from others. I realize, of course, that it
is not much fun to hear all this (especially as most
people prefer to be flattered and to ignore unpleasant truths about themselves), but even if you have
no desire to learn the truth today, one day you will
have to listen. In fact, you are privileged to be able
to learn it here, from me.

Prepare yourselves therefore as I prepare myself, to make reparation for all your mistakes. Let's
suppose that I have been a scoundrel, the worst
kind of firebrand, and that I repent and regret my
past ways, and want to atone for my faults. Let's
suppose that I have wronged every one of you : that
I have defiled, robbed and massacred you all. Well,
just let's suppose ! And now what ? By putting up

with you all, loving and instructing you, I am paying my debt and making reparation. But what if it were not true that I had wronged you in the past? What then? Well, so much the better. This is a question I purposely leave unanswered: I have no obligation to tell you why and how I came to earth, nor where I come from. That is my business. But let's presume that I am someone who has broken all the laws and now I am condemned to pay you what I owe you. There! You like to hear me say these things, don't you?

Well, if I can talk about this without embarrassment why should you not decide to reason in the same way and start atoning for your faults towards your husband or wife, your children, your parents, your friends? Of course, I understand. You prefer to believe that you are blameless whereas I am a confirmed criminal. All right, all right. But is it the truth? No matter! If I am capable of admitting in front of you that I am not perfect, you can do so, too, in front of others.

Someone has a son who is always tormenting him and bringing dishonour on him, and he comes and complains to me, "What have I ever done to God to deserve such a child?" The answer is that you have undoubtedly incurred a debt towards your child in the past, otherwise he would not have been born into your family. Many parents who are just, honest people, have to put up with children who are hooligans. It is really astonishing. In fact it would seem to be impossible according to the laws of nature, they could not have sown such seed, but there is always a reason concealed in the past, for the law is unequivocally just.

Recently a brother came to see me. He was in a great state of anguish because he was unfailingly kind and generous to his family and he received only ingratitude and cruelty in return. The injustice of it was destroying him. So I said to him, "Would you like me to give you a key, an infallible remedy, the perfect antidote? There is one thing you should know, and when you know it, you will never be angry or in revolt again. On the contrary, you will feel fine. That one thing is this: the invisible world is using all these difficulties to make you stronger, to free you, to oblige you to think and become a better human being. What is gnawing at you and making you ill is that you think that the way you're being treated is unjust. Think, instead, that it is just and you'll find that you feel much better." Well he did. He trusted me and he got better and is now radiant and full of peace. He knows that he is almost certainly paying for past transgressions and that idea has saved him. You have to accept to envisage things this way, otherwise the trials and difficulties will end by destroying your digestive system, your heart or your nervous system.

And today I say the same thing to all of you : if the injustices you suffer torment you, accept the idea that there may be apparent injustice, but in reality it is not so. Even if this were not true, the conviction that it is would help you to free yourself, to suffer much less and to become a better person. I have proved the truth of what I am saying, personally. In the past I did not know about this remedy and I often wondered why certain things happened to me. Now I never need to wonder why, I just think that I am getting my just deserts, even if it is not true. What did Jesus ever do to make him deserve crucifixion? Of course, Jesus' destiny was exceptional. Don't imagine that you are in the same situation! And yet, it can happen that the innocent are imprisoned or put to death. If they rebel against the injustice of it, they simply torture themselves to no purpose. Here on earth, even if you are innocent, it is best to think that you are just as guilty as everyone else, for, by thinking this way, you will free yourself.

You have been given the task of discovering within yourselves a spiritual realm governed by immutable laws. The slightest infringement of these laws must be paid for, sooner or later. The thing that puts you off the scent is that payment is delayed. But everything is on record. Every single thing triggers a reaction. You will find this same law in many different areas. Take an example from chemistry: you have to wait quite a long time for a sheet of Litmus paper to turn from red to blue or vice versa. The change comes all of a sudden when just one drop of acid or alkali is added to your mixture. Yes, but that one drop is the last in a whole series. Similarly, if you examine the mechanism of a watch, you will notice that the hands start moving only after several different wheels have begun to move one after another. The time that elapses between the moment when the wheels are first set in motion and the appearance of any visible, tangible result may be long or short, but since the parts are all connected, a result is inevitable.

Suppose that you have a particular vice or passion: you cannot see any immediate repercussions and you continue indulging your passion to excess. This over-indulgence sets invisible wheels moving and they in turn set others and still others in motion until one day, you wonder why you are so ill, so worn out. Your fatigue or your illness started long ago. Today, the bailiff has turned up with the summons, you should have known it would happen! How is it that human beings have not yet understood that law which you must admit, can be found everywhere, on all levels? All their tribulations and misfortunes stem from their inability to analyse and interpret the mechanisms of their own physical and psychic organs.

If you really want to become a son of God, a truly complete being living the life of the soul and the spirit, you have to respect the precepts of moral law. There is no other way. The doors are closed to anyone who transgresses these laws. The hidden world never gives way before the capricious whims of disrespectful, anarchical, degenerate human beings. "The hidden world?" you may ask, "did you say 'hidden'?" Yes, exactly. This world is hidden, invisible, and if you tell me that you cannot believe in something you cannot see, I shall have to answer that you have never learned to reason. Are your thoughts visible? And your consciousness, your opinions, your feelings: are they visible? And all your plans for the future: can you see them? No, of course not, yet you are persuaded that they exist. You are ready to fight and even to kill people to defend your convictions which are invisible, too. Have you never realized that your whole life is based on things you cannot see? Only the invisible world exists for sure: all the rest is open to doubt. If you deny the reality of the invisible world, you are sawing off the branch you are sitting on, and one fine day you will find yourself on the ground! The truth of it is that you deny these realities rather than admit that you have never taken the trouble to examine them for yourself and form a valid opinion: you should be ashamed of such intellectual dishonesty. Someone who denies the existence of the invisible world is signing his own death sentence.

Human beings will continue to suffer until they have understood that the invisible world is the only reality. I have an argument for ignorant people who cannot admit this. You only believe in what you can see, do you? Very well. Suppose that you live in the lap of luxury and one dark night someone seizes you by the throat and says, "Your money or your life!" Well, even if you have never believed in life before, because it is invisible, all of a sudden you begin to believe and you're ready to give up all your visible goods for the sake of something invisible. How inconsequential of you! If you were logical you would say, "Take my life, not my money." But then, of course, you'd be dead and what good would all your money be to you then? You see, nothing is more precious than what you cannot see. Life is an invisible reality and, in spite of that, you are ready to give up everything else for it. How extraordinary human beings are!

Does the invisible world really exist? Does it claim our recognition and respect, like the visible world? Yes, it does and far more so. It is high time you became aware of the existence of that subtle level of life and learned to appreciate it. If you do, you will see what happens within you. Even if other people notice no change, inwardly you will begin to live in freedom, joy, buoyancy and inspiration, your life will become musical and harmonious, you will be living true poetry. And if you reach this ideal it will reflect even on your material welfare. People will begin to see the beauty of the life you are living and the whole world will bring you treasures. For everything is connected: inner wealth attracts exterior wealth, even if it takes time for the effects to show. If you attain that level of perfection in your inner life, your vibrations and emanations will reach the whole world, even the farthest star, and will bring back to you all kinds of blessings and happiness.

A blessing is already being prepared for you, it is on its way and will soon reach you. When it comes, you may question it, "Where have you come from, who called you, and when?" "You did," will be the answer, "a long time ago." Yes, that is how it is. Happiness is on its way, but it takes time to get here for it has to come a long way. Unfortunately, there are also sorrows on their way. You may not realize it, but you called them to you a long, long time ago. Besides, what else could someone who is sombre, ignorant and stupid expect? Glory? Dazzling light? A visit from an Archangel? Impossible! Why? Because he is incapable of attracting such splendour: there is a law of affinity which the Initiates of old concealed in the saying "Birds of a feather flock together." This proverb contains a vast science, incomprehensible to primitive men. They could not understand the law of correspondences (also called the law of affinity, the law of the echo, the boomerang effect or the law of polarity) so the Initiates preferred to launch it in the form of a popular saying, a piece of folk-lore.

"How could I have brought all this misfortune on myself?" you ask. "By your attitude, your way of thinking and your behaviour," reply the Initiates, "it was inevitable." "And my good fortune?" "You have worked hard, made sacrifices, been generous...." It is absolutely just. Heaven does not ask your opinion about what reward you would like: you are given exactly what you deserve.

7

NATURE'S MEMORY

Every living being, in fact everything in creation, has a duplicate copy and everything you think, feel, say or do, you do in duplicate. If you help someone or if on the contrary you injure him, the original action disappears into the past but it leaves its imprint on you in the form of an exact copy. Here again, I am telling you an essential truth that humans are totally unaware of, they never think that what they do for good or for evil has repercussions that reach far beyond the original act. Fortunately or unfortunately, it does not end there, fortunately if what they do is good, and unfortunately for them if what they do is wrong.

Everything that exists in nature therefore, plants, insects, animals, the stars or the mountains, all have a duplicate. For the time being, we shall concern ourselves with human beings. Clairvoyants are able to see a person's etheric double, which has exactly the same form and functions as his physical body. In fact, if the etheric body or double is disconnected from the physical body, the person loses his perception of pain, you can prick, burn or hit him, he will feel nothing as long as the etheric body is separated from his physical body. However, even though it has gone out of the physical body for a time, the etheric double is always in touch with its physical counterpart by means of the silver cord. It is only in the event of death induced by illness, a wound, or a severe shock, that the silver cord is broken.

But it is not only the physical body which has its counterpart: the astral and mental bodies also have theirs. The double of the astral body provides energy on the level of feelings and the mental body provides energy on the level of thought. If a man's astral double detaches itself, he becomes emotionally numb and indifferent, and incapable of any reaction of sentiment or emotion. Similarly, if his mental double detaches itself, he becomes incapable of thinking. These phenomena are still relatively unknown and unexplained. If doctors and psychiatrists knew them they would find an explanation for many psychological disturbances which have always seemed inexplicable. The trouble is that they look for explanations on the physical level, whereas more often than not they lie elsewhere.

But let us talk about this question of duplicates. You all know that in government or business offices, when an official document, a decree or ordinance, is prepared, there is always a carbon copy or a photocopy: the original is sent to the person or office concerned and the copy is kept on file for future reference. It was not humans who first invented filing systems or memory-banks for their records, but nature itself. Nature keeps a copy of all your actions on file in her archives. And when we move on to the other side and seek admission into Heaven, we take with us the copy – or rather the three copies: physical, astral and mental – which bear the record of all our deeds, thoughts and feelings. The originals have gone who knows where, far away to some other planet or to the stars... you cannot get them back, it is too late. But a certified copy is always on file in your own, inner archives.

When a human being reaches the other world he comes before an assembly of highly evolved spirits who remain with him while he watches the projection of the film of his life on earth. The film is not shown for their benefit: they do not need to be shown his life-story, they know it already. They already know the degree of evolution he has reached, his sins and crimes as well as his good deeds. It is the man himself, poor creature, who needs to see the film, for he is so ignorant he does not know himself. He imagines that he was either a monster or a divinity and as he is apt to be mistaken in both cases, he has to be shown exactly what he was.

It is we who need to learn something, not the entities of the invisible world, and that is why it is we who keep our files within us, so that we can take them with us when we leave this life. Whether you believe this or not will not alter the reality, these are facts and will remain so whatever you choose to believe. Of course, it is more reasonable to believe me and to accept the truth, because then you can correct your mistakes and improve yourselves. I am convinced that if everyone knew these vital facts there would be very few who would choose to remain prisoners of their own weaknesses, but as they know nothing of these things they go on living as they have always lived, with no inkling of the consequences of their behaviour. And this is why it is so important to instruct human beings, especially children, and tell them about the laws. Even if they do not really understand what you tell them to begin with, later on they will stop to think about it and, above all, they will have an opportunity to verify the truth for themselves.

What happens, for instance, when someone commits a crime? Why is it that he is pursued by a memory which keeps flashing the same picture onto the screen of his mind and never leaves him in peace? The crime is over and done with, a thing of the past. He has nothing to fear since he has left no visible clues behind him. Ah, yes, but the duplicate copy is still with him and he has no idea how to get rid of it. So you see, there is no need to go to great pains to study all the sacred books of humanity to find out about these things. The truth is demonstrated every day within each one of us. Why does a man's conscience continue to reproach him with the memory of his crimes to the point that he loses his appetite and cannot sleep at night until he has made reparation? Simply because everything is on record in his innermost being.

Cosmic Intelligence has had plenty of time in which to adjust everything and order the universe with wisdom. It is only in the minds of men that everything is disordered, chaotic and meaningless. It does not matter what you explain to them in this regard, all they say is, "Oh, no. I don't believe it." But who do they think they are, to allow themselves to say such a thing? If they are so intelligent, how is it that in their daily lives they are so puny and weak, so utterly powerless to change the course of events or even to extricate themselves from their worries and troubles?

So, as I have said, everything is recorded. To know this law should be enough to convince you that you should be very careful not to indulge every passing fancy. Every bad thought, even if it only passes through your mind, leaves an imprint on you which will be with you for all eternity, all the more so because once a negative imprint has been made there is a tendency for it to become a pattern which repeats itself over and over again indefinitely. I have often talked to you about this and explained how you can create new patterns in yourself which will end by replacing the old ones: the bad habits acquired in the past. If you do nothing to substitute good patterns for the bad ones, they will stay with you, time and again, in every reincarnation. You must erase them, otherwise there is no reason why they should not reappear each time. Hold on to your good patterns, your qualities and virtues, and work at improving them (there is always room for improvement), but you must also work at correcting your defects.

Human beings often get discouraged because they have no idea how to set about correcting their faults. They spend years struggling against a bad habit, acquired God knows when, and never manage to rid themselves of it. In point of fact, instead of fixing all their attention on a defect, which is the negative result of some destructive act in the past, it would be far better to concentrate on what they can do to build the future. From now on, therefore, say to yourselves, "Now I'm going to make amends and rebuild," and each day with unshakeable faith and tenacity and absolute conviction, work to this end. Take all the elements God has given you, your powers of imagination, thought and feeling, and concentrate on projecting into yourself the most beautiful pictures. See yourself bathed in music and light, see yourself in the sun surrounded by forms of the utmost perfection, imbued with qualities of kindness and generosity, with a capacity to sustain others and to help and guide them.

Since everything is recorded, you must record only the best possible material. You will see for yourself that if you begin this work, you will be so taken with it, so busy and inspired, that it will become an inexhaustible source of joy to you, for you will be building the Temple of God within you. I know of no endeavour more worthwhile than this: to build the Temple of God in one's innermost being, using all the best materials: utterly disinterested thoughts, feelings and acts.

Most human beings are very far from entertaining this ideal. All they are interested in is to record a little interesting information in their brains, without getting down to the real work. The difference between our Teaching and all other schools is that in the schools you *learn*, whereas here you *work*. Information can be useful but it does not transform you. Only the work we do ourselves is capable of transforming us, not what we have read or heard. Knowledge can incite us to start working, but we shall never be transformed if we make no move to set certain forces in motion within us. If we fail to

act on what we learn we shall always be the same
however vast our learning.

Of course, it is true that you do learn something
here in the Universal White Brotherhood, but the
important thing you receive is the stimulus to start
working at your own transformation. You cannot
transform your whole being unless you raise yourself to heights beyond your own limits every day, to
find the materials you need. Just like a bricklayer,
a mason or a master builder, you have to go out
and get your building materials. Some of you will
say, "But I don't get any pleasure out of this
work!" and with this remark, of course, they show
exactly what class they are in. Every creature in
nature falls into a certain class. According to their
tastes and tendencies they have found their shelter
or their lair, they have chosen their skin, hide, fur
or feathers. This is destiny. And one day nature
will put us into a certain class, too, according to
our preferences and the choices we have made.

In fact, man's destiny is determined by the nature of his needs. For example, if you need alcohol
and drugs, if you need to frequent night-clubs every
night or to spend your time gambling, your destiny
is already traced out for you in advance: moral de-
gradation, financial ruin and possibly prison. And
if you need to contemplate divine beauty or to
spread peace and light all around you, there, too, it
is self-evident: you will meet happiness and fulfil-

ment. How is it that people have never noticed that every need or wish, every desire they harbour, sets them on to corresponding rails which lead automatically either to regions infested with hornets, snakes and wild beasts from which no one escapes intact, or on the contrary to luminous, magnificent regions where all is joy? Man determines his own destination by his own inclinations, tastes and desires.

Some are predestined to be ill, some to meet with failure, others are predestined to be ill-treated victims, and in each case it is they who have determined or predestined themselves. You ask, "Is there any way of escaping one's destiny?" and I am obliged to answer, "No, there isn't. Not, at any rate, during your present incarnation. If you had been intelligent and reasonable in your previous incarnation you could have arranged things much better for this one. Now what you can do is to use all the tremendous possibilities open to you to make your next incarnation a success – and this you can do only by working day and night at making new recordings, preparing new patterns."

I am well aware that what I am talking about now is very difficult to achieve. How can we summon up enough good will and energy from within to undertake and to persevere in such a task? And although your task begins with yourselves, whatever good results you achieve will in the long run reflect favourably on the whole world. All your other work, all your material activities, however skilfully they may be planned and executed... God knows if they are really any use to other people! All is recorded, filed and computerized and, in the end, when a man dies and goes over to the other side, the heavenly entities he meets do not even ask any questions, "How have you lived? What have you done? Did you help or comfort anyone, did you guide anyone towards the Eternal Fountainhead?" They never question a human being because they know in advance that he would lie, no, they take a tiny reel of film from him, put it on their projectors and let him see it for himself.

You will think that this is impossible. Not at all! Everyone of us has a tiny reel, an atom, lodged at the point of his heart and which contains a recording of every detail of his life. Look at a magnetic recording tape: you have a length of tape and you cannot see or hear anything on it, but put it into the appropriate machine and what do you hear? The Barber of Seville! To make sure you do not start inventing all kinds of stories and trying to justify yourself, you are told to sit down in front of a screen and keep quiet while the film unwinds. And you see everything, absolutely everything you have ever done down to the last detail. History does not relate how your hair stands on end at the sight of it! "But you have no hair left then! How can your hair stand on end?" Well, of course, you have left your physical hair behind, but you have another kind of hair and, I assure you, it does stand on end! And there you are: there is no way of bluffing or lying about your life.

Although it is not explained in quite the same way, all this can be found in the sacred books of humanity and, in particular, in the Egyptian Book of the Dead. In this book it says that when a man dies he comes into the presence of Osiris, his soul is weighed, and so on. There is also the Tibetan Book of the Dead which reveals the different stages of a soul's journey in the after-world, how he is judged and the conditions imposed on his rebirth.

Well, there you have a few words on the law of memory or records. What matters now is to realize how important it is for you to make new and better recordings, better patterns for yourself, every day. What about the old ones? Little by little you will superimpose your new recordings on the old ones and they will be erased. This is a prospect that should encourage you.

Unfortunately, for a long time you will still go on recording a lot of worthless material because you will continue to follow the old patterns still in you. But at least be aware of what is happening so as not to allow your situation to get any worse: as soon as you realize that you have recorded something undesirable, react immediately and make amends so as to prevent bad consequences. If you have had spiteful thoughts about someone, or hurt him with your words or if you have destroyed something, be aware of it at once and correct it. For the time being this will be the most you can do, but at least do that! I have noticed that some people do nothing, absolutely nothing to make amends for a negative thought or act. Whereas others at least recognize their fault, "It slipped out. I couldn't control myself." This can happen to all of us, but we must notice it immediately and try to make amends.

8

REINCARNATION

I

Today, I would like to talk to you about Rein-carnation, because I have seen that this subject is on your minds, it worries you. You were always told that man lives once and once only, and now you find it hard to accept the idea of Reincarnation.

I could go at length into the way the Egyptians, or Indians, or Tibetans thought about Reincarnation, and what they did to verify it, but for the moment I will be content to give you a few interpretations of the Gospels, proving that Jesus believed in Reincarnation. You say you have read the Gospels through and through and have never seen the word Reincarnation. My answer is that there was no reason to mention it at that time, because everyone believed in it. How were the Evangelists to know that one day people would no longer believe? To them, it was tradition, and therefore not essential to their already condensed records. You say you are not convinced? You will be very soon.

Let us look in the Gospels at some of the questions and answers exchanged between Jesus and his disciples. Jesus asked one day, "Who do men say that I am?" What does this mean? Do you know anyone who asks others to tell him who he is? People know who they are, they don't need to be told by others; for Jesus to have asked such a question means that they believed in Reincarnation. And the disciples answer this, "Some say that thou art John the Baptist, some Elias, and others Jeremiah or one of the Prophets." Without Reincarnation, could Jesus be someone who had long been dead?

Another time, Jesus and his disciples encountered a blind man. "Master," the disciples asked. "Who did sin, this man or his parents that he was born blind?" Unless it refers to Reincarnation, the question is absurd. When was the blind man to have sinned, in his mother's womb? Was he able to spend nights carousing, or stealing, or murdering? Either the question is implying a past life or it is meaningless. You say, "Well yes, but the disciples were reportedly plain uneducated fishermen, wouldn't they be apt to ask odd questions?" In that case, Jesus would have reprimanded them, he does so throughout the Gospels... but here he simply answers, "Neither he nor his parents sinned." The disciples wondered whether the son was born blind as a result of the sins of the parents, because they knew from the Hebraic law that every infirmity, abnormality or calamity, is the result of that person having transgressed the law unless... and this was also possible... that person was paying for someone else. One never knew on sight therefore, whether a person's misfortune was due to his own sins, or to the fact that he had sacrificed himself for someone else.

This was the accepted belief among the Jews. The disciples asked the question because they knew that no one would be born blind without good reason, and not, as Christians are told, simply because it pleases God. Jesus replied, "Neither hath this man sinned, nor his parents, but that the works of God should be made manifest in him." That is, so that Jesus would heal his blindness, and as a result, all who saw him do it would believe in him. To the disciples Jesus said: you have been taught that there are two reasons why men suffer, either because they have sinned and are being punished, or they are free of sin and are paying someone else's debts in order to hasten their own evolution. But there is still another category of people, those who have finished their evolution and do not have to return to earth again, who are free, but who nevertheless do return, accepting to endure suffering, disease or infirmity, even martyrdom, in order to help mankind. The blind man belongs in this category. "Neither hath this man sinned nor his parents, but that the works of God should be made manifest in him." Such a person saves quantities of people.

If you are still unconvinced, here is another argument: one day Jesus heard that John the Baptist had been thrown in prison. The text says simply, "Now when Jesus had heard that John was cast into prison, he departed in Galilee." Sometime later, John was beheaded by order of Herod. After the Transfiguration, the disciples asked Jesus, "Why then say the scribes that Elias must first come?" and Jesus answered, "Elias truly shall first come and restore all things. But I say unto you that Elias is come already and they knew him not, but have done unto him whatsoever they listed. Likewise shall also the Son of man suffer of them." The text adds, "Then the disciples understood that he spoke unto them of John the Baptist." It is clear that John the Baptist was the reincarnation of Elias. Furthermore, it says in the Gospels that when the angel appeared to Zacharias, the father of John, to announce that his wife Elizabeth would bear him a son, the angel added, "And he shall walk before God in the spirit and power of Elias."

Now let's see what the Prophet Elias had done to deserve being beheaded when he returned to earth as John the Baptist. It is an interesting story. Elias lived at the time of King Ahab whose Queen, Jezebel, was the daughter of the King of Sidon. Because of Jezebel, Ahab and all his people believed in Baal and worshipped that god. Elias was sent by God to reproach Ahab for being unfaithful to the God of Israel, and told him, "As the Lord God of Israel liveth before whom I stand, there shall not be dew nor rain these years but according to my word."

Elias then went and hid in the mountains as God ordered him, to avoid capture. At the end of three years, the country was ravaged by drought and famine, and the people were starving. Again God sent Elias to King Ahab. When Ahab saw him, he cursed him bitterly for causing the drought. "No," said the Prophet. "I have not troubled Israel, but thou and thy father's house, in that ye have forsaken the commandments of the Lord and thou hast followed Baal. Now therefore, send and gather to me all Israel unto Mount Carmel, and the prophets of Baal four hundred and fifty... which eat at Jezebel's table." When they were all assembled, Elias told them they would now see who was the real God. "I, even I only, remain a Prophet of the Lord, but Baal's prophets are four hundred and fifty men. Let them give us two bullocks and let them choose one bullock for themselves and cut it in pieces and lay it on wood, and put no fire under; and I will dress the other bullock and lay it on wood and put no fire under. And call ye on the name of your gods, and I will call on the name of the Lord, and the god that answereth by fire, let him be God."

The prophets did as he said and all morning long they invoked the name of Baal, "O Baal, hear us!" There was no answer, and Elias mocked them, "Cry louder... for either he is talking or he is pursuing, or he is on a journey, or perhaps he sleepeth and must be awaked!" The prophets cried all the louder, and because they had some knowledge of magic, they slashed their bodies, hoping that the blood would attract evil spirits and elemental forces that would set fire to the altar. Nothing happened. Elias decided that was enough. "And Elias took twelve stones according to the number of tribes of the sons of Jacob... and with the stones he built an altar in the name of the Lord, and he made a trench about the altar... and he put the wood in order and cut the bullock in pieces and laid him on the wood, and said: Fill four barrels with water and pour it on the burnt-sacrifice and on the wood." Now all was ready, and Elias the Prophet called upon God, "Lord God of Abraham, Isaac, and Israel, let it be known this day that Thou art God in Israel and that I am Thy servant, and that I have done all these things at Thy Word. Hear me, O Lord! Hear me, that this people may know that Thou art the Lord God!" Then the fire of the Lord fell from Heaven with such power that everything was consumed, nothing was left, neither victim, nor wood, nor stones, nor water. The terrified people fell on their faces in recognition of the real God, the God of Elias. Whereupon Elias, somewhat overzealous after his victory, led the four hundred and fifty prophets to a mountain stream and slit their throats.

That is why Elias had to face being beheaded... it is the law. Jesus referred to the same law when Peter took his sword to cut off the ear of the Caliph's servant in the Garden of Gethsemane, "Put up thy sword into its place, for they who would take the sword shall perish with the sword." The truth of these words is not always demonstrated in the same life... how did Elias die, for instance? Not only was he not beheaded, but a chariot of fire was sent to carry him up to Heaven. It was later that he paid, when he came back as John the Baptist. Jesus knew who John was, he knew what his destiny was, and he said those magnificent words about him, "Among them that are born of woman, there has not risen a greater than John the Baptist." But he made no attempt to save him, he did nothing because he knew that justice must take its course. Now you see why Jesus left the country: he was not meant to save John the Baptist. The law is the law.

Now let us go still further. I will show you that nothing makes sense without Reincarnation,

nothing in life, nothing in religion. Ask a priest or
pastor what makes one person rich, handsome, intelligent, strong, successful in everything he undertakes, and another one sickly, ugly, poor and miserable and stupid: he will answer that it is God's
Will. They may talk about grace and predestina-
tion, but that doesn't clarify things, and in any
case, it is always God's Will. If you analyse it, and
since God has given us a mind, why let it rust...
then God is capricious. He has whims that make
Him give everything to one person and nothing to
another. Very well, I accept that, He is God and it
is His Will, He is magnificent and I bow to Him.
But the thing I find incomprehensible is that He
should be angry and offended when people to
whom He has given nothing make mistakes, when
they stop believing in Him and turn to crime. If
God gave them so little intelligence, so little heart,
why does He punish them for what they do?

God, Almighty and Omniscient, could He not
make everyone good, honest, wise, intelligent, de-
vout, and wonderful? Not only is it His fault if
there are crimes, but He punishes people for committing them! I cannot go along with this. I agree
that God is all-powerful, I agree that He should do
as He sees fit, He is irreproachable, but then, why
is He not also consistent, logical, and just? The
least He could do is leave humans alone, but no,
He sends them to Hell for all Eternity. That

astounds me. For how many years did they sin, thirty, or forty? Well, let them remain in Hell forty years, no more... for all Eternity, I cannot go along. If you think about it... but people don't dare to think, their minds are clouded over by all they've been taught. If it is wrong to think, of what use is the mind? God gave us a mind, He must want us to use it.

When we learn to accept and understand the idea of Reincarnation, then everything changes. God really is the Master of the Universe, most great, most noble, most just, and it is our fault if we are miserable and unhappy and stupid, our fault if we didn't know enough to use all that God gave us from the very beginning and had to make our own costly experiments. As God is also most generous and most tolerant, He lets us do as we wish, he says to Himself, "Well, they will suffer and run into trouble, but it doesn't matter, I will always have more love and more of everything to give them when they are ready for it... they have enough reincarnations ahead in which to learn...." He leaves us free, whatever happens to us is our fault. Why does the Church put all the blame on God? You answer, "The Church doesn't blame God, it simply abolished the idea of Reincarnation." It comes to the same thing, if you think about it.

The Christians believed in Reincarnation until the fourth century, as did the Jews, Egyptians, In-

dians, Tibetans, etc.... But no doubt the Church
Fathers said to themselves that this belief gave people too much time, they were improving too slow-
ly, and if the idea of Reincarnation was eliminated
they would improve more quickly, they would
have only one life in which to become perfect!
Gradually the Church invented more and more
dreadful things to frighten people into obedience;
by the Middle Ages, all they believed in was devils,
Hell, and everlasting damnation. Belief in Reincarnation was abolished so that people would be
forced to improve through fear and dread, but not
only did they not improve, they became worse...
and ignorant to boot! We must recover this belief,
for without it nothing is true, nothing in life makes
sense, God is a monster of cruelty.

The question of Reincarnation has been dealt
with scientifically, many people have remembered
living in a certain place at a certain time, numerous
books have been written on the subject... about the
way the Tibetan lamas choose the Dalaï-Lama for
instance, and one really extraordinary case I knew
about when I was still in Bulgaria. A couple came
to the Fraternity, worried about their child who
said things that were incomprehensible. "One day
we took our child for a walk," they told us. "And
although he had never been there before, when we
got to a certain place he said at once that he knew
it well, and had been there many times." Now

these parents had had a previous child, who always accompanied them. "Don't you remember?" the child went on. "This is where I hid so as not to go to school, and there is the river where I drowned!" It was true that their first child had drowned in that river, but no one had ever told this child about it. Clearly their first child had come back to reincarnate in the same family, which is rare, but it has been known to happen. Some children remember their past life up to the age of seven, but their mothers, instead of listening, are apt to give them a slap and tell them to stop talking nonsense. After one, two, three attempts, the child gives up and doesn't talk about such things anymore.

Now you see that although the word Reincarnation does not appear in the Gospels, it was common belief at that time, part of the tradition. Here is another example. Jesus said, "Be ye perfect as your Father in Heaven is perfect." What are we to think? Either Jesus was being thoughtless in asking common sinners to attain the perfection of their Heavenly Father in the space of a few years, or he didn't realize Who his Heavenly Father was... in either case, it is not flattering for Jesus! Actually, he was talking about Reincarnation. Jesus certainly didn't believe that anyone could become perfect in one lifetime, but he knew that if you long for perfection, and work toward it during one incarnation after another, you will finally reach it.

What does Moses say in the Book of Genesis when describing the Creation? "And God said, let us make man in our image, after our likeness: and let him have dominion over the fish of the sea and over the fowl of the air and over cattle... God created man in His image, in the image of God created He him." What happened to the word "likeness"? God doubtless intended to create man in His image and in His likeness, that is, perfect like Him, but He did not, He created him in His image only, He gave man the same faculties as Himself, but not the fullness of those faculties, that is, the resemblance. An acorn is the image of its father, the oak tree, it has all the same possibilities, but it hasn't the likeness, it does not resemble the oak tree until it has been planted and grows up. Man is the image of God, he has been given the same wisdom, love and power, but in such infinitesimal degrees compared with the Wisdom, Love, and Power of God! In time, when man develops himself, he will resemble God, and he will possess all of God's virtues in abundance. Do you see now how this progress, this passing from image to resemblance cannot take place without Reincarnation? God said, "Let us make man in our image and after our likeness," but He didn't do it. "God created man in His own image, in the image of God created He him."

Moses revealed the idea of Reincarnation in the omission of the word likeness and the repetition of the word image.

But people don't know how to read what is written in books, or in the great Living Book of Nature, which is full of references to Reincarnation. A tree, for instance, only the Kabalists have really understood the meaning of a tree: they symbolized the Universe as a tree on which every living creature has its place as part of the roots or the trunk, as leaves, or flowers, or fruit. This vast and comprehensive science says that all existence, all activity, all regions, have a place on the Tree of Life. At different times of the year, the leaves, flowers and fruit fall to the ground, where they decay and become fertilizer for the roots. It is the same for humans: when a man dies, he is reabsorbed into the Cosmic Tree, and then later he reappears in the form of a branch, or a leaf, or a flower. Nothing is ever lost, beings appear, disappear, and reappear ceaselessly on the wonderful tree that is the Tree of Life.

So you see, Reincarnation is engraved on everything, everywhere in life. Where else? In the phenomenon of evaporating water. Water evaporates out of the ocean into the air, where it turns to snow or rain, and then falls back into the ocean. A drop of water doesn't disappear, it travels all over the world, rising high into the sky and falling back

down on mountains and valleys, sinking deep
down into subterranean stratas, changing color as it
goes, from yellow to red to green. Water rising and
falling is a phenomenon that proves the law of
Reincarnation, a spirit is like a drop of water jour-
neying all over the world, learning how to be perfect.

Another example? Here is one : when you go to
bed at night, you take off your clothing, one by one
you set aside your jacket, your shirt, your sweater,
etc.... Nighttime and going to sleep are symbolic of
dying, the clothing you shed represents the different bodies you shed, first the physical, a week or so
later the etheric, and lastly the astral, which takes
longer because it is the seat of our passions and desires. The astral plane and the lower mental planes
are the region we call hell, where we must remain
until we are purified. Not until we are free of the
mental body can we enter Paradise, the first heav-
en, the second heaven and the third heaven... seven
heavens in all according to tradition. Only when
we are stripped of everything and are completely
naked, that is, purified and free of all impediments,
do we enter the seventh heaven of Paradise.

Morning symbolizes birth, the return to earth.
Once again you put on your clothing, your shirt,
sweater, jacket, etc.... When he is to be born, a
child must clothe himself in each one of his divine
bodies, then the mental body, the astral and etheric

bodies, and finally, the physical body. You see, every night of your life, you have undressed and every morning you have dressed, without realizing that you were imitating the motions of incarnation and disincarnation. If we could interpret our little daily habits, our behaviour and work, what it means to eat, to breathe, etc... we would make many discoveries. All the great mysteries of the Universe are reflected in our acts, in our speech and gestures, only you have to study in an Initiatic school to know how to decipher them.

Some people are waiting for the Church to pronounce itself officially on the subject of Reincarnation, but when will that be? I have had the opportunity to talk occasionally with prelates, and I know that many of them believe in Reincarnation, but don't dare admit it for fear of repercussions. In any case, I say that unless you accept this idea of Reincarnation, you will never be able to understand the things that happen to you, why you are in a certain situation, why you are hounded and mistreated, or on the contrary helped and encouraged, and you will never know what to do, how to prepare for your next life. How far can you go without the Truth?

II

When we read the lives of the saints and Prophets and Initiates, we wonder why they had to suffer, what they had done to deserve martyrdom. The reason must be sought in their past lives, for even when we re-establish the divine order within ourselves, it doesn't mean that we have paid our debts, or that our past life is erased. We have to pay down to the last penny before we can be entirely free.

Take the disciples. They were with Jesus constantly, they lived in the Light and followed the divine Teaching, they harmed no one, what had they done to deserve being thrown to wild beasts or massacred and why did Jesus do nothing to help them? He did nothing because he knew they had not finished paying their debts. In other incarnations they had no doubt committed a few sins, and in their ignorance, omitted to make the necessary reparations before they left for the other side. It is said, "Let not the sun set on thy wrath," and "Before the sun set, go and forgive thy brother." But no one really understands what that means: taken literally, there isn't much time to make amends, especially in winter when the sun sets early! But here it is not the sunset of the physical plane. In the symbolic language of the Initiates, "sunset" means death, the time when man must depart for the other side. He is given plenty of time, but once the time is up, if he has forgotten to pay or if he hasn't known that he must settle his debts before the sun sets, then the law of Karma goes into effect. Everything we do is inscribed, everything leaves an imprint that hardens and crystallizes, there is no "getting round it," as they say: you must pay and whether you settle all your debts before the sun goes down or not, you will still have to pay every penny.

You who receive spiritual Teaching, who live in the Light, even you are not completely protected. You have debts whether you are in an Initiatic school or not, and you will still have accidents or run into difficulty and trouble from time to time... no matter whether you follow the Teaching and are in the Light or not. Is it clear that the results of the good you do now are not for this life but for the future? Whenever you have trouble, when you have a problem, you should accept it, and say, "Lord God, I know that nothing can undo the work I have done in the Light. If I have difficulties now, it means I am being given the chance to liberate myself. I know that, and so I accept, I do not ask to be spared."

You say, "Since Jesus was crucified, does it mean he had a Karma to pay?" No. For Jesus it was different... here we are touching on the question of sacrifice. There are beings who offer to sacrifice their lives, who suffer pain and hardship even when they have nothing left to pay, but they are exceptional. People make errors of judgment when they don't know the details of Reincarnation.

From the point of view of Reincarnation, people can be divided into four categories. In the first group are the ones who have no consciousness, knowledge, light, or morality, who break every law, commit crimes, and run heavily into debt. When they reincarnate, they come back under difficult conditions and have to suffer in order to pay and make the necessary reparations. Their lives are not happy ones.

In the second group are more evolved beings who try to develop the qualities and virtues that will lead to their freedom. Even so, it isn't possible to settle all one's debts in one incarnation; they must come back again to complete their task. This time they will be given better conditions, they will be allowed to be useful on a higher plane, but they must still come back until their debts are all settled and they are free.

In the third group are beings who have reached a high degree of evolution, but who return to earth to accomplish specific tasks. They have very few debts, and are given a great deal of time in which to use their higher consciousness to do good. Once their mission is accomplished these beings do not need to return.

Some of them however, and this is the fourth group, once they reach the state of permanent happiness and felicity and unlimited freedom next to God, are so filled with compassion for suffering humanity, that they leave the heavenly regions of their own accord, even if it means being tortured and killed. Others in this group who are not obliged to return, can – if they wish to continue a spiritual task they have begun – instil or implant themselves in another being who is highly evolved. Jesus referred to the possibility of such unification when he said, "If a man love me, he will keep my words, and my Father will love him, and we will come unto him and make our abode with him." These beings do not actually reincarnate, they have no physical body of their own but become part of someone else, and go through his life from conception to maturity, working through that person.

Everyone wants to be free, but they don't understand what will make them free: it is not by avoiding obligations or shirking their duty or severing all their ties that they can be free. Freedom comes from having paid your debts... in full. People want freedom from their wives, from their children or the boss, or society, or from life itself, by suicide. But dear brothers and sisters, there is no such thing as freedom until you have paid all your debts and your Karma is effaced. Freedom is desirable, but only in accordance with divine law. It is rare to find someone who knows how to acquire freedom. Even here in the Fraternity, some of you think you become independent by avoiding your obligations, as if you went to a restaurant and ate a huge meal, and then left without paying. It is not honest, not right or noble, the luminous spirits on the other side do not allow that attitude. People think they will be free once they leave their wife, or their boss, but actually it is the way to create new problems, new traps will lie in wait for them to show them how mistaken they were. In the end they are caught between Scylla and Charibdis!

The best way to liberate oneself is to be loving, and the worst way is to go on being selfish, crafty, calculating and stingy. Every time you show generosity and kindness, every time you give, every time you sacrifice yourself, you work toward your liberation. That is why, instead of holding on to your possessions, always calculating the risk of giving and dodging the issue... give! Look at the way people act toward each other when there is divorce or separation... how tightly they cling to their "share"! They don't know that because of this attitude, they will have to meet again in similar circumstances in a future incarnation.

It is love, generosity, kindness, forgiveness and mercy, that permit the disciple to liberate himself. Of course if you talk this way to the average person, you will pass for an idiot, most people are lacking this Light, they don't know that there is a reason for being generous and kind.

Initiates know the deeper reason for things, they realize how worthwhile it is to give, to help, to be generous and large, and to share, for that is the way to freedom. So... give! Give more than justice requires, in that way you will be free even more quickly!

III

It happens with nations and peoples as it happens with human beings and all creatures: they are born, they expand, and when they reach old age, they must yield their place to others... they follow the same curve, giving what they have to give and then dying away as though they went to take a rest before coming back with more treasures and wealth. This is the way with nations, we have seen it, and also with religion: religions come into being, their influence is widespread, they rise to great heights, to the culminating point... and then wear out, they lose the key to life and become crystallized. This is what happened to the great Mysteries of the Temples of ancient Egypt, to the hierophants that held the key, the power, the knowledge, the science... where are they today? They all followed the immutable law of life: everything and everyone that is born, dies and yields its place. Only that which has no beginning has no end.

Take Greece, past and present... the quantity and the quality of creative artists that came out of Greece in the past... poets and writers, painters and sculptors, philosophers... all highly gifted. A country is like a river: the river bed never changes but the water flowing in it is always fresh, always changing. The inhabitants of the river are the countless drops of water that come and go on their way to the sea while millions of other drops take their place. When they reach the sea and are warmed by the sun, they become light and subtle enough to rise into the atmosphere and wait until it is time for them to come back in the form of rain or snow, to join the torrents and rivers and go coursing down the mountains and through the valleys. Everything flows and fluctuates.

A country is a river in which people come to reincarnate from many different places and at different times. Or it is a house which is occupied for a number of years by one group of tenants, and then new tenants move in... for years the house was filled with the atmosphere of song and music and harmony, but now, with the change of tenants, the atmosphere is entirely different, more prosaic and turbulent... the house is the same house, but the atmosphere that affects it is different. A country's destiny can be explained in the same way: Greece is still the same country, but the inhabitants are different from the ones who lived there three thousand years ago... and the same for other countries.

You ask, "Why are some people, like the Tibetans for instance, able to hold on to the same concepts and traditions and customs for thousands of years?" Because what happens is the same as what happens in the human organism: the cells are constantly renewing themselves, they change, but they continue doing the same work. Or like a factory where the personnel is changed from time to time, some workers are let go and others take over their work, but the new worker is already trained and knows what is required of him. Spirits who reincarnate in Tibet are already trained in Tibetan ways; they have an affinity for Tibetans, and are prepared to live there. And Tibetans who are prepared to be like the French, reincarnate in France; there are many former Tibetans in France, even here in the Fraternité.

You ask, "What about the Jews that have been persecuted for so many centuries?" The Jews who were persecuted and martyrized were spirits from many different countries who reincarnated into Jewish families because it was their Karma to be persecuted or massacred, but they hadn't necessarily always been Jews. Heaven arranged for them to be born into a Jewish family at a certain time so that they would pay their debts. And the same in Greece, spirits came from elsewhere to reincarnate there, perhaps from Bulgaria, because the two countries have always hated each other and people often reincarnate near to their former enemies. Many Greeks have reincarnated in Bulgaria, whether as a reward or as punishment... I don't know.

Whether you hate or love someone, it is the same thing, you create a link with him. Hatred is as powerful a link as love : if you want to be free of someone and never see him again, neither hate nor love him, simply remain indifferent, for if you hate him you will bind yourself to him with unbreakable chains... for centuries to come. This is something you should know. People think they are cutting themselves off from a person if they hate him, but on the contrary, hatred binds you to the person you hate. Like love. The difference being that the bonds of hatred bring you something quite different from the bonds of love... but just as surely and powerfully. If all the nations of the world knew this, they would see how ridiculous and dangerous it is to hate each other.

You mustn't be surprised or annoyed if I say that France is doing everything to make her lose her great men. The world has been given a wealth of treasures in the past by the genius of French artists, writers and philosophers ; but if France contin-

ues to cut herself off spiritually from Heaven, from
God who distributes these treasures... then the ge-
niuses will go and incarnate somewhere else. Great
spirits are universal, nations fight over them, but
they don't care about their nationality; if you ask
them, they say, "We belong to the Universe, our
country is the Universe." Can't you see the Ger-
man and French soldiers who died in the wars between their two countries meeting on the other side
and having a drink together, laughing at how stupid they were to have killed each other... when
they were all sons of God?

It is simple for the invisible world to make one
country go downhill and another one evolve. Why,
for what reason? Their sense of justice. Look at
Bulgaria for instance: a few centuries ago, it was a
miserable downtrodden country that never pro-
duced anything in the way of thinkers or artists or
scientists... and now all that is beginning to change,
everything is improving. Neither the glory of a
country nor its decadence last forever. And what
about China, how many centuries has it taken
China to stir itself from sleep and come abreast of
the times? Now that it is beginning to rouse itself,
the rest of the world is frightened! How do you
explain that, who determines things like that, and
for what reason?

It is the Heavenly Hierarchies above who make
those decisions. For them it is easy, like giving aid

to underdeveloped countries. If a country is poor and backward, one of the richer, more advanced countries sends in a team of economists and technicians of all kinds... a few years later country is on its feet. The invisible world does the same thing, it dispatches engineers and scientists, that is, a team of specially chosen souls, with the responsibility of starting a whole new culture. Sometimes all it takes to set a country right in very little time, is one really good political leader.

It may make you unhappy to hear me say that your country is going to be shaken by events, but I am stating a fact, I have no interest either way, being neither Bulgarian nor French... I am a citizen of the Universe, I belong to the sun and not the earth, why would I fight for any of them, Greece, or France, or Bulgaria, as long as I am above all frontiers? I do say however, than the Slav scientists have gone further in the field of parapsychic discovery than anyone else... telepathy, psychometry, clairvoyance, radiesthesia... they have even succeeded in photographing the aura! In spite of appearances, in spite of the way it looks at the moment, Russia will one day abandon its philosophy of Marxism, and the Communists will become Brothers of the great Universal White Brotherhood.

What the Russians have discovered so far is very little compared to all that I have revealed to you over the years. I predict that this science, the

Initiatic Science, will spread all over the world...
not of course, the highest degrees of the science,
not the ultimate secrets, for humans are not ready
to know the whole Truth yet. Human nature uses
discovery as the means to profit or to dominate the
rest of the world. For that reason there will be a
limited amount revealed to them. But certain
truths will be brought to light and the whole world
will know them, it will be the Solar Culture.

IV

"Every flower that comes up out of the ground is linked to everything else in the Universe, Nature can withhold her support if the flower appears too early, before its time, and if Nature is against it, the flower dies.

"For each one of you also, all Creation had to consent to your arrival. You say, "But I am no one, why would Nature be concerned with my birth?" Because it is so. Every detail, including the amount of food and drink you will consume during your lifetime, is noted down somewhere, and for you to appear when you did, the Cosmic budget must have had room for you at that time. Everything is connected to everything else, every living thing is part of the Cosmos, and nothing can appear in Heaven or earth without the common consent of all Creation...."

I know this idea will surprise you and perhaps shock some of you, for it is not the usual way of

looking at things. People believe everything happens by chance, that nothing is intentional or fore-
seen and there is no presiding Intelligence to make
decisions... which is the reason people do not understand the things that happen in the world.

Take a tree, for instance. All Nature must agree
to participate in its development before the tree
can grow and bear fruit, it cannot exist unless the
elements it needs are supplied by the earth, water,
air, sun, and heat... and human care. A tree needs
the help of all Creation, but as this action is imper-
ceptible, the tree is thought to be there simply by
chance. A man also exists, breathes and moves because he has the help of all Creation, if a single element is withheld, if he is denied air, or water, or
vitamins and hormones... he dies. Where do these
vital elements come from? From the Universe, in
its willingness to participate.

For a man to arrive on earth... do you think it
simply happens, like that, by chance? Human ignorance is unbelievable! Is that the way it is in the
world, in families, in government, in business?
"Well," you say. "There are special people to calculate expenses and establish the budget, to figure
out how much to spend on food, on heat, on up-
keep, on where to cut down, which people to let go
and which new people to hire...." Well, do you
think there is no one to plan or approve each person's arrival on earth? Why would everything be

done intelligently and according to plan in cities and families, and stupidly, vaguely, left to chance in the Universe? Human ignorance is indeed abysmal!

The fact is, there exists above, an extraordinarily well-planned, well-balanced economy which determines the number of people that are to come down on earth, when they are to come, and how long they will remain. Every human need is provided for, prepared in advance for each person, yet people think it all happens haphazardly, that even for someone like Jesus, no one took care of selecting the exact moment that he was to come, no one calculated the most favourable astrological aspects... and so Jesus happened to come along, no one quite knows why. No, his coming was predetermined by the most magnificent beings above. Nothing is ever left to chance. Even for Hitler, it was determined that he would come in order to teach certain people a few lessons and be taught a few himself in the process.

You ask, "How can they foresee everything like that above?" If I told you that it is all figured out automatically by computers...! For humans didn't invent computers, Nature has been using them for ages. The Cosmic computer contains the essential information on each person including his past, and on the basis of that information, it issues a statement saying when and in which country each per-

son will be born, with which body and what kind of
mind and faculties. Other spirits are assigned to see
that these decrees are carried out and that everything takes place at the proper time. If an accident
is scheduled, they watch and wait for the precise
moment, and then provoke the accident! People
think it happens by chance, but the fact is that
everything is calculated ahead of time with mathe-
matical precision. If a child is to be born at a certain time, the electronic machines determine with
precision the sign of the Zodiac under which he
will appear, the position of the planets, etc... and
the child is born as scheduled. Everything is calculated on the basis of his past incarnations, even the
hour of his conception, and whether he will be
happy or unhappy, rich or poor, whether he will be
injured at a certain moment or not... all according
to what he has done during his past incarnations.
Everything is automatic, his birth, his death, and
all other events and circumstances of his life.

"But then what about liberty?" you ask. Liberty is in the spirit, liberty is present whenever the
spirit manifests itself, when it decides to alter the
given processes, to improve or accelerate them. But
on the whole, life is released and set in motion the
way a mechanism is, like a child's electric train
that runs along the tracks and stops at stations,

coming to a final halt when the child doesn't wind it up. Man also runs down and comes to a stop; if he is not wound up again, he dies. Man is a machine that is set to operate for a certain length of time, he runs into obstacles and goes through little tunnels like the child's electric train, according to plan. Even chance meetings are planned: when you meet someone "by chance" who changes your whole life, it was planned that way, and when you fall in love "all of a sudden," it was planned before you were born. A little baby lying in its crib already has all the equipment he needs for life stored within him... he is a factory inside, a state, a constellation... a whole world in himself!

Would it surprise you to hear that for just one little flower to grow and blossom, the whole Universe must consent unanimously to help it, and contribute to its needs... otherwise it dies? This is true for you also: if you are given favourable spiritual, mental, and material conditions in which to live, you are able to grow and flourish, whereas with other conditions you are hindered and unable to develop. Sometimes conditions that are favourable to others are detrimental to you, or conditions that are detrimental to others are wonderful for you; you may be gifted with all kinds of qualities and intellectual faculties, but be lacking in something else, health for instance. All because some of the forces and currents in the Universe were not in accord with your coming into existence, and they make trouble.

That is why you must work on harmony, you must try to be harmonious as the stars and everything else in the Universe, otherwise someone or something will always be causing you trouble. You may be in perfect harmony with all your family and neighbours, but perhaps there are other people who wish you harm... and so your life will have some unpleasantness in it, the good will be mixed with bad. That is the reason I am so insistent on your being in a state of harmony with the entire Cosmos... so that you will have an ideal life, filled with nothing but beauty and light. You see, you haven't understood yet how important the exercises are that I have given you; if you don't know certain things, the details don't seem important, but once you know the whole truth, you recognize their value.

Another example: suppose you have a friend whom you like, who really helps you... but there is someone else on another level who dislikes you, who is your enemy... with that person you have nothing but arguments and bitterness and grief, and with the other, you have a wonderful time. Both are part of your life, both affect you, but the enemy creates trouble. That is why it is important to be in harmony with the whole world. It is difficult of course, but you must try: first of all, try to be in harmony with the entities above who direct your life, and then try to mend things with those who hate you, so they will stop doing you harm. That is the reason for the saying, "Let not the sun go down on thy wrath... before the sun set, go and reconcile thyself with thy brother...." Here "sunset" means the end of this incarnation, because later on, it is much harder to make reparations. In this life, we must go and find our enemy and settle our dispute, pay what we owe, and then live in peace. Each bad thought, each bad feeling and bad action is harmful, there is no "getting around it," these are living entities and there is no use pretending they don't exist, they do exist, and sooner or later, they will find you and do something to harm you.

Now let us look for a moment at this idea of our destiny being determined ahead of time. As I have already said in one of my other lectures, we have the opportunity before we come down to earth of changing certain things, providing the Heavenly Hierarchies allow us to, but once we are born, we no longer have that possibility, our lives must unfold as planned, and our entire organism, our nervous, muscular, circulatory systems, our bone structure, our health and our intelligence, all are part of our fixed destiny. If we are born ugly or deformed, we will not have as much in the way of joy, happiness, or success, as for instance, a girl who is born beautiful, gifted, and full of charm. Her destiny will be quite different, she will be chosen "Miss World," she will be besieged by photographers and invitations, she will become a star, and a handsome multimillionaire will want to marry her!

That is what I mean when I say that you cannot change your destiny in this incarnation, but if you start to work now on the next one, if you hope and ask and pray for the next one to be different, it will be. During this incarnation you will be limited, but in the next one, you will have everything you long for. Those who don't know this, reincarnate in exactly the same situation.... Why do you suppose some people are in dreadful situations? It is because they didn't know how to work in their previous lives, what to work toward, what virtues to develop, what opportunities to ask for in the next life. They were ignorant in their past lives, and if they go on being ignorant in this one, the next incarnation will only be another failure.

You should listen to me, dear brothers and sisters, listen and take advantage of what I am telling you, resolve to spend the rest of your life thinking about it, hoping and asking for the best things, because in that way, you project ideas that will later crystallize, materialize themselves. Your present form is crystallized, it resists change, in fact it cannot change or be replaced until it has served its time. But when a man dies, the things he has created in his mind become concrete, they crystallize on the physical plane, and he comes back to earth with all the beauty, intelligence, health, and goodness he thought about. His desires materialize in a new form which is as resistant to change as the old one, and resistant also to all destructive and negative forces. Whatever we do now will bear fruit in the next life. Many of you come and tell me, "Maître, I have worked for years on myself, but there are no results, nothing is changed. I am the same as always." And I answer, "You don't understand. Actually you have changed certain things, but you have to wait, your present form must disappear before the new form can appear. When it does, then you will see the fruit of your hard work, and you will be astounded by all its beauty and splendour."

Earlier I told you that freedom belongs to the spirit, and now I want to explain that. If you observe an animal's behaviour, you see that it is subject to the natural laws, it is not free to choose whether or not it will oppose things or try and change the course of its life... animals have not that gift. They obey, they submit, they are true to the natural laws and for that reason they are innocent even though they are destructive... when they leap on their prey to kill it, it isn't their fault, but their nature urging them on. A child is a little animal

too, he obeys his instincts and follows his impulses
without using his mind or his will. Not until later
will he have the opportunity to oppose Nature,
when he is allowed to choose whether he will live
in harmony with these laws, or break them.

Now when a man does no more than eat and
sleep and enjoy himself, when he has no other goal
but to earn his living and put children into the
world... whatever he may imagine, he is living the
life of an animal, a life governed by instinct, a vege-
table life... and animals do as much. His life proceeds in spite of his consciousness or his will, almost independently of him, and he goes from
childhood to manhood, to old age and death, without having had much to do about it.

But when a man begins to use his mind consciously, to control his life and purify it and add to
it the spiritual element, then he becomes a power
factor, he has the power to change his destiny.
What is destiny? Destiny is an implacable chain of
events, causes and consequences to which all life is
subject as long as it is purely animal, biological, instinctive. For instance, what is a hen's destiny?
Can a hen become king, a poet or musician? A
hen's destiny is the casserole! All creatures have
their own particular destiny... a wolf's destiny is to
be hunted, to be caught and killed, or carted off to
a zoo; and lambs and doves also have a destiny in
conformance with their life and the elements that
formed them.

To escape destiny, you must overcome weakness and stop submitting passively to a life filled with things over which you have no control... breathing, eating, procreating, and sleeping... that kind of life is far from the divine life. It is divine in that it comes from God, but it is not divine in the spiritual sense. The divine life begins when a man realizes he is made of more than flesh and bone and muscle, that he is not all stomach and sex but also spirit, and that he is meant to act and create in the spiritual realm and devote his life to something more, something sublime, luminous, and divine. Then yes, he escapes his destiny, but not completely. The destiny of falling ill and being left in a cemetery to rot... that destiny is fixed (I am speaking for the physical plane), and there is nothing one can do. But the spiritual life gives us an opportunity to add something more to the instinctive life, and to reach a higher plane, beyond destiny. In order to do that, the spirit must be allowed to manifest itself and leave its imprint on your life, to intervene in everything you do. In that way, you avoid your destiny and enter another realm, where Providence reigns. The destiny of the body is to return to dust and ashes, but not the spirit, spirit has no destiny, it comes under the heading of Providence.

How can we come under the heading of Providence? By realizing that between destiny and Providence lies free will, and that the whole point of be-

ing a disciple is to free the will, to be able to move
and work and be active in the spiritual world.
When the disciple comes under the influence of
Providence, he is given a wide variety of choices,
he can choose whenever he wishes, and his choice
will always be wonderful; whereas when he was
under the control of destiny, he had no choice,
there was only one path leading to destruction, disintegration, disappearance. What is an ox's destiny? To be harnessed to a cart and made to pull it
to the end of his days, poor thing, or be cut in
pieces and sold to the butcher. Oxen can do nothing about their destinies, nor can any of the animals. Nor can man, unless he has this knowledge;
without this light, he too is limited by destiny, he
too is subject to being kicked about and oppressed.
If he comes under the control of destiny, even a
king or emperor can do nothing, destiny is inexora-
ble and must be fulfilled. And so, the heads roll
under the guillotine. Destiny is extremely difficult
to avoid, for most people have created heavy Kar-
mas for themselves in their past lives. The law of
cause and effect is absolute, destiny is unconscious
and without pity, as infallible as a law of physics: if
you hit a glass, it will break. The laws of destiny
are equally infallible.

We have every opportunity in this incarnation
to create good conditions for the next one, providing we know what to do and do it consciously; if

we do not work in that direction in this incarnation, the next one may be worse than this one. The Church, when it took away the promise of Reincarnation, took away the chance for people to improve themselves. Christians have no idea of their potential. They are told that when they die they will go to Heaven (provided they attended mass regularly) and be seated on the right hand of God. On the other hand, if they have neglected the Church, they will burn in Hell forever and ever... why does the Church deceive people in this way? To comfort them? It would be more comforting to tell them the truth.

To summarize: all creatures (and there are many) who let themselves be dominated by their instincts and their physiological needs, who do no spiritual work, will never be able to change their destiny, their lives will unfold as decreed. Those who work ardently and do all they can to enter the world of love and light, will escape. Destiny is indeed cruel and relentless, but they will no longer be subject to it, they will live in more subtle regions, and receive all the beneficent elements that neutralize harmful influences. It is still destiny if you will, for Providence is destiny, but another kind: everything is set and determined, but divinely!

There. What I have just told you is very important. Now you know that if you content yourself with living like the rest of the world, without doing anything on the higher planes, you will not be able to change your destiny nor create your future life, since you submit to the way things are. Perhaps you will have a good destiny, it may appear that way... the "destiny" of people who live in the midst of wealth, for instance, surrounded by luxury and protection, with nothing to disturb them while they eat and drink, marry and have children, and travel the world over... a splendid life! But not in the eyes of the Initiates. Other people who have to fight for the Truth and work and suffer and run into obstacles, who have very little in life, actually are better off than the ones who seem to have everything.

Humans are apt to have a materialistic idea of happiness and are encouraged in this by astrologers, who tell them such things as, "Oh, this is wonderful, you have Jupiter in the second house, the Sun in the tenth house, Venus in the seventh... which means that you will be rich and important, famous, happy in love, and have everything you want...." If they see squares and oppositions, they are sorry for you. Because they don't understand! An Initiate would never read a horoscope that way, he would look to see if you are ready to work spiritually, if you are capable of obeying God and carrying out His divine plan, and then he doesn't bother with squares and oppositions, or planets in exile, etc....

But this light, this different way of interpreting things, is not the way our contemporary astrologers, who are slave to the ordinary way of thinking, who judge the way everyone judges, and believe with everyone else that the real life is based on material wealth and success. But all that is temporary, and what happens when it disappears? The true value of a horoscope is not discernible to everyone. Others may cry out in admiration over someone's horoscope that I find mediocre; I look and see that this person will never do anything important for Heaven, nothing. Some people have what is considered a "brilliant theme," with signs of wealth, talent, position in society, etc., and I see them as most ordinary, insignificant people, I would never want to be in their place nor have a "good" horoscope like theirs. I follow other rules for judging a horoscope that astrologers know very little about.

I could point out other things that would show you how little astrologers really understand these things. Instead of saying you are running into debt on a certain plane and explaining to you how you can pay and be free, they tell you how to avoid an accident that is supposed to occur on a certain date... which is useless advice, for if the accident is to occur, it will occur whether you go out that day or not: Karma, which is not to be put off, not to be tricked, will see to it that the accident occurs on the day before (or the day after) it was scheduled.

You ask, "But then, what good is astrology if it doesn't help you to change your destiny?" It does help, but not that way. It would take too long to explain, but here is an example : let us suppose you learn that at a given moment in your life you will have to pay a certain sum, and that if you don't pay, your furniture and all your goods will be seized, you will be evicted from your house, and out in the cold, at the mercy of the weather, you will be faced with illness. Rather than standing by doing nothing but wait for the fatal day, you decide to prepare for the eventuality by working and saving, putting aside as much as possible with the result that when the day comes, you have the wherewithal to pay and you are not evicted. You can apply this image to any phase of life, an accident, an illness, a business collapse, anything that lies in wait for you.

And so, my dear brothers and sisters, today I have given you some truths that are absolute. Go ahead and study these things for yourselves, you will see that I do not deceive you. Ahead of you lies a tremendous opportunity, because you have this Teaching to help you, to prepare you, to tell you how to create a future for yourselves that will be truly glorious.

Distributed by:

BELGIUM: Mrs Brigitte VAN MEERBEECK
Chemin du Gros Tienne, 112
B - 1328 Lasne-Ohain

BRITISH ISLES: PROSVETA Ltd.
4 St Helena Terrace
Richmond, Surrey TW9 1NR

Trade orders to:
ELEMENT Books Ltd
The Old Brewery, Tilsbury, Salisbury
Wiltshire SP3 6NH

CANADA: PROSVETA Inc. - 1565 Montée Masson
Duvernay est, Laval
Que. H7E 4P2

FRANCE: Editions PROSVETA S.A. - B.P. 12
83601 Fréjus Cedex

GERMANY: URANIA
Steindorfstraße 14
D - 8000 München 22

GREECE: PROSVETA GRÈCE
90, Bd. Vassileos Constantinou
Le Pirée

ITALY: PROSVETA
Bastelli 7
I - 43036 Fidenza (Parma)

PORTUGAL: Ediçãoes Idade d'Ouro
Rua Passos Manuel 20 – 3.° Esq.
P - 1100 Lisboa

SPAIN: PROSVETA ESPAÑOLA
Caspe 41
Barcelona-10

SWITZERLAND: PROSVETA Société Coopérative
CH - 1801 Les Monts-de-Corsier

UNITED-STATES: PROSVETA U.S.A.
P.O. Box 49614 Los Angeles
California 90049

Any enquiries should be addressed to the nearest distributor

NOTES